A WELSH COAST TO COAST WALK

Rhinog Fach from Y Llethr

A WELSH
COAST TO COAST WALK
Snowdonia to Gower

by

JOHN GILLHAM

CICERONE PRESS
MILNTHORPE, CUMBRIA

© John Gillham 1996
ISBN 1 85284 218 0
A catalogue record for this book is available from the British Library

Acknowledgements

I would like to thank those who have helped me in the production of this book. Roy Clayton was a good companion on the long walks, as were Van Greaves, Graham Buckley, Ken Garrad, James and Sherrill Clayton on the shorter trips. Lowe Alpine have supplied good quality clothing which kept me comfortable and safe on the hills. Thanks must go to Welsh Water for the supply of information and historical photographs of the Elan Valley. Cledwyn Fychan of the National Library of Wales discovered a good account of highwaymen on the Rhinogs. Thanks to the walkers who have walked Snowdonia to Gower and kept me in touch with the changes. Last but not least, special thanks must go to my wife, Nichola, who wasn't with me for the original book but has kept me company on recent forays for all the new routes.

Front Cover: On the slopes of Yr Aran looking down on Nantgwynant

CONTENTS

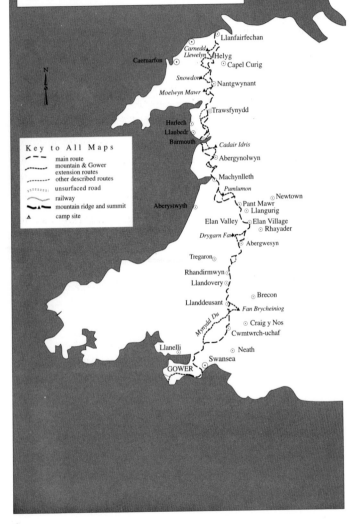

Snowdonia to Gower
A Welsh Coast to Coast

Key to All Maps

- — — — main route
- ·–·–·– mountain & Gower extension routes
- - - - - other described routes
- ……… unsurfaced road
- ∿∿∿∿ railway
- ▄▟▙▜ mountain ridge and summit
- ▲ camp site

Llanfairfechan
Carnedd Llewelyn Helyg
Caernarfon Capel Curig
Snowdon Nantgwynant
Moelwyn Mawr
Trawsfynydd
Harlech
Llanbedr
Barmouth *Cadair Idris*
Abergynolwyn
Machynlleth
Pumlumon Newtown
Aberystwyth Pant Mawr
Llangurig
Elan Valley Elan Village
Rhayader
Drygarn Fawr
Abergwesyn
Tregaron
Rhandirmwyn
Llandovery Brecon
Llanddeusant *Fan Brycheiniog*
Craig y Nos
Mynydd Du Cwmtwrch-uchaf
Llanelli Neath
GOWER Swansea

INTRODUCTION

Since the inauguration of Tom Stephenson's Pennine Way in 1965 a great number of long distance footpaths have been devised and written about - some official routes having been adopted by local authorities or the Countryside Commission, others purely informal. Increasing numbers of people have been turning to the fells for recreation. Long distance walking is a natural extension of that challenge - a marathon, a test of endurance. But it is more than that: it takes us to remote, dramatic places where beauty is the norm, gives us the chance to watch the sun go down behind alpine crests, ready to taste our camp-cooked food and then sleep under the stars.

I was first persuaded to go fell walking by my nephew, now a fellow writer, Roy Clayton, who had already been bitten by the bug after a few excursions with his school. His boundless enthusiasm was infectious and I was soon browsing through Ordnance Survey maps planning future expeditions and building mental pictures of mountainscapes from the contour lines. I do not know if I was inspired by my Welsh ancestry or by childhood memories of camping in Llanrwst, but in September 1981 we both completed a coast to coast walk of Wales - from the Irish Sea to the Bristol Channel. It was a memorable experience and although there were times when the spirits were dulled and dampened by aching limbs and lashing rain, there were those of exhilaration - the feeling of relief when first discarding heavy rucksacks (you feel as if you can run a hundred yards in ten seconds, although I have never tried to prove the point); the camp on Drum in the Carneddau when inverted cloud dissipated leaving the flickering lights of the North Wales coastal towns visible in a fading sunset; and the moments of triumph when inhaling the salt air of Gower and looking out to the sea at journey's end. These are memories that linger!

The trip however illustrated to me the need for a comprehensive guidebook. For the route I had chosen, and which had looked so good on the map, was inadequate in many places, especially when passing through Central Wales. Footpaths had become dilapidated through neglect or were obstructed by barbed wire fences or locked gates. Others crossed ground that was unacceptably boggy or rough. There was little useful literature on anything other than Snowdon and in this light I decided I would research and write my own book.

Having done the route once I knew that a north to south journey through Wales' magnificent land, if the awkward sections were improved, must rank as one of the best walks in Britain. Although Offa's Dyke is such a route it does not reveal the character evident in the more rugged heartlands: the best way would surely be through the mountains.

In planning my route, the objectives were as follows:

1. to find an interesting starting point and memorable terminus on the north and south coasts respectively.
2. to find a safe route intimate to the mountain scenery that is synonymous with Wales, and easily negotiable by the heavily laden mountain camper.
3. to keep the distance short enough to enable a reasonably fit fell walker to complete the walk within the confines of a two-week holiday.

I have often climbed to the summits of the Snowdonian mountains whose towering grey ramparts had, on those early childhood visits, seemed so unyielding. Although much of their mystery has been unveiled by my forays, their harsh majesty remains undiminished. Memories of these magnificent peaks are interlaced with those of secluded high tarns lying in the dark quiescence of their ice-sculpted corries.

For all the grandeur of Snowdonia's alpine scenery the moorland peaks and cwms of Central Wales seem to me to be almost as appealing. The landscape is simpler in form, but generally it has been less spoiled by man and its remoteness lends a tranquillity seldom equalled. There are countless upland valleys with chattering crystal streams verged by coarse, pale mountain grasses and scattered resilient wind-thrashed rowan trees, which in late summer display vivid scarlet berries. The vast open spaces of this area known as the Elenydd have been divided by monotonous and insensitively planned conifer plantations and embellished with large reservoirs. These additions are not universally popular but few can dispute that the Forestry Commission provided greatly improved access to the lonely hills and provided much needed employment and income for the local inhabitants.

The Elan Valley reservoirs have had eighty years in which to blend with their environment. This they have done admirably and although the huge stone-built dams contradict the theme they are so impressive when the overspill waters thunderously cascade down their walls. Further south, those who pass through Rhandirmwyn on the southern edge of the Elenydd will surely wish to return and explore fully this miniature Snowdonia boasting a myriad oaks and many clear trout-filled rivers, which meander through steep sided stony hills to reach the verdant pastures of the Tywi Vale.

The entry to South Wales is marked by a return to high mountain country but this time very different in character. The Black Mountain (or Mynydd Du as it is known in Wales) is at the western end of the Brecon Beacon Range and similarly consists of old red sandstone. Glacial action has formed magnificent cliffs on the northern and eastern faces of the group and also provided two lovely tarns Llyn y Fan fawr and Llyn y Fan fach. By comparison the country passed to the north-east of Gower is dull but the aesthetic quality is restored on that coastline finale!

And so we have a personal itinerary for a coast to coast walk - one that can be completed piecemeal or in one go (about a fortnight). Whichever way it is undertaken the route will be well remembered for its varied and stimulating scenery. I would like to think that in highlighting lesser-known areas the book will encourage a greater awareness of the beautiful landscapes and interesting places outside Snowdonia. In this the Welsh have surely undersold themselves, choosing instead to invest in the propagation of the already thriving north coast resorts, central Snowdonia and the Pembrokeshire coast.

The authorities should also defend the heritage of the rest of the principality with a little more vehemence for, far too often, spectacular views are marred by unsightly ill-planned developments that would stand no chance of being passed in other National Parks such as the Lake District. Can you imagine the Central Electricity Generating Board being allowed to erect a line of electricity pylons in Langdale? Well they have across the Northern Carneddau! There would be a public outcry if Keswick were to become as dilapidated and uncared for as Bethesda (just a few miles from Snowdon!) so why not in Wales?

For all its faults Wales is a grand place with a great diversity of scenery. Each mountain range has its own appeal and character - the lofty whaleback ridges of the Carneddau; the bold serrated ramparts of the Glyders; the sheer majesty of Snowdon, truly the monarch of Cambria; the gnarled and faulted flanks of the heather-clad Rhinogs and the wild rolling Elenydd moorlands that rise to their zenith at Pumlumon.

The mountains are divided by many fertile vales sheltering pleasant villages, which make good havens for a night's rest. Indeed on such a walk memories of the high fells are enriched by those of convivial evenings at the local pub and the kind and interesting people met. One of the most vivid reminiscences of my first walk across Wales is of being lifted by a superb hot drink at Llandovery's Coffee Shop after being soaked by heavy driving rain, which had lasted all morning. I had anticipated with trepidation the crossing of the Black Mountain escarpment but, as I sat staring out of the window, a shaft of sunlight pierced the gloom and someone at the next table commented that the weathermen had forecast sunshine for the next two days. I knew then that I would complete the walk and the discomfort disappeared with the sighting of widening blue skies.

This walk across Wales is therefore a journey of contrasts. Contrasts of scenery and weather, of high windswept moorlands, craggy mountain ridges and idyllic wooded valleys; of industry, folklore and legend. It provides scope for personal variation according to weather and mood. Wales has a lot to offer those who are willing to explore the landscapes far from the roadsides and what better way to spend a holiday than to don your boots, shoulder your sac and set out on this grand journey from coast to coast through one of the most delightful mountain regions of Britain.

Six Years on
Since the publication of my original *Snowdonia to the Gower* (Diadem Books) developments have made changes necessary. The impending privatisation of the Forestry Commission means that free access cannot to be taken for granted; a new road in Swansea and a dubious development of nearby Valley Wood into a theme park meant

wholesale changes to about 15 miles of the route had to be made. This does mean that you get to see the seaside a bit earlier - at Black Pill in the Swansea Bay. In this new book I have also offered more low-level alternatives in Central Wales; after all, who wants to be on top of Pumlumon, Drygarn Fawr or the Black Mountain in mist and driving rain?

Many who are familiar with the original book will see that I have now divided the walk into twelve sections rather than eleven. Although they were just for the convenience of the book layout the "valley centres" were a little too far for some, especially around the Rhinogs and the Black Mountain. Stopping short of the Black Mountain means that the route down to the Swansea Valley the next day is unnecessary. I therefore decided to show a new route across the entire 'ridge' - east to west and added a very interesting and seldom walked low-level alternative through the isolated limestone defile of Tyle Garw to Cwm-twrch Uchaf.

The changes reduce the length of the walk but, for the masochists among you, there is now a Gower extension from Three Cliffs Bay along the spine of Cefn Bryn to the beach at Rhosili.

Tryfan from Helyg

Looking back to the sea from the first day's walk ,Wyn Anafon, Anglesey and Puffin Island

CHAPTER ONE

Across the Carneddau
Llanfairfechan to Helyg

The peaks of the Carneddau, Wales' great northern range, are, in the north, smooth-profiled grassy giants interspersed with the occasional rocky outcrop. Further south, near the Ogwen Valley, they display rugged cliff-ringed cwms, the Black Ladders (Ysgolion Duon) and Craig yr Ysfa being two of the greatest cliffs in Wales.

Llanfairfechan, a Victorian coastal resort, where our route commences, lies in the shadow of the steely grey scree slopes of Penmaenmawr Mountain, whose form has, over the years, been disfigured by extensive quarrying to provide material for road building.

The town's intimacy with the mountains makes it an ideal starting point and within half an hour of leaving the stony seashore we are on the rocky crest of Garreg Fawr, gateway to the higher peaks which are spread out to the south. The delights of striding on the lofty ridges of the Carneddau are sampled en route to Drum, where the high-level alternative parts company.

On a bright summer's day many walkers will opt to continue along the high route and scale the 3,000-footers that bar the way to the Ogwen Valley, for these mountains and their high connecting ridges are a joy to walk. In less friendly conditions, however, most will opt to descend to the more sheltered lower route which descends to Pen y Castell then threads its way through the desolate cwms of Dulyn and Eigiau. Ruined dwellings are testaments to the plight of those who tried and failed to scrape a living from these infertile soils.

On both routes the amiable descent to Ogwen, at the end of a long day, will be remembered for its panoramic views of the peaks of the Glyder group - Tryfan, Glyder Fach and, at the head of the valley, Y Garn.

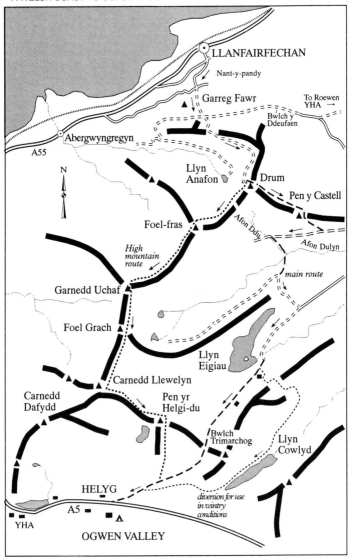

LLANFAIRFECHAN TO HELYG - The Main Route

There is a temptation on leaving Llanfairfechan's high street to make a bee-line for the mountains but if one were to take a strictly purist view of a coast to coast walk the starting point would have to be the beach.

A short stroll on the resort's stony shores, inhaling fresh breezes from the Irish Sea, would make a fitting appetizer before heading south beneath the new coast road then up the lane towards Nant-y-felin. The lane twists to the right climbing on the lower slopes of Garreg Fawr which towers above it, obscuring the greater Carneddau peaks. As it levels off, another lane doubling back (east) up the hillside is taken before turning right on a southbound farm track (GR 682739) which takes a steep line up the western flank of Garreg Fawr giving fine views of Llanfairfechan and Anglesey.

On reaching the top of Garreg Fawr, the rocky crest of Tal y Fan, most northerly of Wales' 2,000ft mountains, comes into view. The southern landscape is badly scarred by rows of unsightly electricity pylons which lead the eye to Bwlch y Ddeufaen, a pass between the peaks of Tal y Fan and Drosgl. A few yards beyond the pylons the path is traversed by an old Roman road leading to Roewen to the east. From Garreg Fawr the route continues along a cart track which ascends the ridge to Drosgl and Drum. The track switches to the western side of the ridge high above the hollow of Llyn Anafon, which sits on a grassy shelf above the river it feeds, dwarfed by the stony fellsides of Llwytmor, Foel-fras and Drum. In views to the north-west the Afon Anafon meanders gently between pale hillsides and disappears from view by the distant stony slopes of Foel-ganol and the dark conifer forests of Aber.

There is an ethereal quietness on the Northern Carneddau seldom experienced on other Snowdonian hills, and this is particularly evident on the enclosed approaches to Drum. This vast untamed mountain wilderness is now less populated than at any time since the Bronze Age.

Drum's summit, where the cart track terminates, is an airy place with good views of the lush Conwy pastures, Llandudno's Great Orme and the Isle of Anglesey, though Foel-fras obscures the Snowdonian giants from view. A circular stone shelter will offer respite from hostile elements.

We now descend the slopes of Foel Lwyd for Pen y Castell, a pleasant heather-clad rocky top overlooking Cwm Dulyn. By continuing eastwards and keeping to the right of the wall encountered halfway down, we meet the footpath at GR 732688 without the need for crossing fences or walls. Follow the path south-westwards to a stile and sheepfold by the Afon Ddu then head downstream.

The river crossing on a bridge over the Dulyn Intake (where water is conveyed via a tunnel to Llyn Eigiau) precedes a grassy path which rises south-westwards to meet an old farm road. This threads through a strangely contrasting area - overgrown with ferns and thistles. Twisted hawthorn trees grow from bouldered slopes and dilapidated dry-stone walls surround small, ruined smallholdings.

A water company service road descending from Melynllyn lake is met as the path climbs into Eigiau. First glimpses of the shallow reservoir are seen as the road is followed eastwards to its junction with the terminus of a metalled road. From here a rutted track leading on directly to the Eigiau Dam is followed as far as a stony track at its southern end. This passes below Hafod-y-rhiw, a charming white-walled dwelling in marvellous surroundings. The immense crags of Eigiau rise at the far side of the lake, while the view south-westwards reveals the peaks of Pen yr Helgi-Du and Pen Llithrig-y-wrach, separated by the pass, Bwlch Trimarchog, which is the gateway to the exit from the Carneddau peaks.

The route diverges from the cart track south of the reservoir (GR 719641). Here a grassy, reed-lined track leads to the disused farmhouse of Cedryn. A collapsed wall can be followed to Bwlch Trimarchog on an otherwise trackless stretch on rough grassy terrain. Above, on the slopes of Pen Llithrig-y-wrach, are the redundant workings of slate quarries, but the chief point of interest is the gigantic crag Craig yr Ysfa at the head of Cwm Eigiau.

The upper slopes to Bwlch Trimarchog are quite steep but safe except in wintry conditions (see alternative route) but the collar work is rewarded by first glimpses of Moel Siabod which towers above Capel Curig and the wooded hillsides by Nant Gwryd. Snowdon and the Glyder summits are obscured by Pen yr Helgi-Du's southern arm, Y Braich. The retrospective northern views show Craig Eigiau slightly obscuring Llyn Eigiau while in the distance the Conwy Valley meanders to the horizon and the Irish Sea.

From Bwlch Trimarchog the descent into the grassy hollow formed by the Afon y Bedol is trackless until the point where the river, a farm road and a leat all converge. At this point trace the left bank of the leat, which veers to the right on the low slopes of Y Braich. Tryfan's shapely profile is revealed as the path nears Tal-y-braich-uchaf. The leat can be crossed by a footbridge at GR 606700 from where a path descends to the Tal-y-braich farm road which leads down to the A5 at Helyg. Gwern-y-gof Isaf farm, one of the finest mountain campsites in North Wales, is situated on the south side of the road a mile to the east.

Diversion avoiding Bwlch Trimarchog
In hostile conditions, Bwlch Trimarchog can be avoided by a low, slightly longer, route along the shore of Llyn Cowlyd. From Llyn Eigiau instead of passing below Hafod-y-rhiw farm take the road leading to it. The footpath beyond threads through crag-studded, heather slopes before descending to Llyn Cowlyd's barren shore via Garreg-wen farm.

The reservoir is sandwiched between Pen Llithrig-y-wrach's featureless eastern escarpment and Creigiau Gleision, whose rocky-crested ridge commands far more attention despite its inferior height. The path climbs to Bwlch Cowlyd, where fine views of Ogwen are revealed, and crosses marshy grasslands on a westerly course towards the Afon Bedol and thence south-west to reach the farms of Tal-y-braich, where a lane leads down to the A5 at Helyg.

THE HIGH MOUNTAIN ALTERNATIVE
Those who encounter clear weather and decide to stay on the high Carneddau will be rewarded with many grand landscapes on a free-striding ridge walk of epic proportions.

The way from Drum to Foel-fras, the most northerly Welsh three-thousander, is straightforward following either side of the ridge wall. The summit is featureless. A little south of Foel-fras the wall ceases to be useful as it angles sharply towards Cwm Dulyn.

The vast plateaux that lie between here and Carnedd Llewelyn are devoid of distinguishing features and present stiff navigational tests in misty conditions. The north-west slopes gently fall to the wild upper reaches of the Afon Goch Valley, guarded on both sides by the ragged crests of Bera Mawr and Llwytmor. On the other side of the ridge the convex slopes prevent views of the lonely mountain tarns of Dulyn and Melynllyn. A cairned path leads to the rock-strewn summit of Garnedd Uchaf, which provides a good viewpoint. The attention is initially drawn to Yr Elen, a well-sculpted, scree-strewn mountain on the western arm of the giant Carnedd Llewelyn. The westerly aspect is focused along the barren valley of the Afon Caseg which leads down to the town of Bethesda flanked on the south by the Penrhyn Slate Quarries.

The grassy eminence between Garnedd Uchaf and Carnedd Llewelyn is Foel Grach. An obvious track ascends to this summit, to the north of which lies a mountain refuge hut (usually equipped with first aid supplies), for the use of travellers caught in extreme conditions.

After a slight depression the climb continues on a broad grassy ridge that rises to the huge flanks of Carnedd Llewelyn, third highest peak in England and Wales and the highest outside the Snowdon group. The summit, crowned by a couple of shelters and a cairn, is a vast rock-scattered plateau with fine views of most of Snowdonia's principal peaks. The impressive south-western panorama is fronted by Carnedd Dafydd with its sheer northern cliffs - The Black Ladders (Ysgolion Duon). Behind Carnedd Dafydd is the Glyder range, and beyond this are Yr Wyddfa and Carnedd Ugain, Snowdon's two highest tops, looking from here like twins.

The main route traversing the Carneddau continues south-west to Carnedd Dafydd and Pen yr Ole Wen. This would be a feasible way for lightly equipped walkers and when climatic conditions are good. They would also be rewarded with striking views of Tryfan and the Glyders on their descent down Pen yr Ole Wen's East Ridge (avoid the tortuous screes of the south side) to the eastern end of Llyn Ogwen but this descent is steep and arduous, coming at the end of the day and probably best avoided by those with heavy rucksacks. A halfway alternative takes the amicable slopes leading down to the Ogwen Valley at Bodesi from Craig Llugwy.

Probably the best way on from Carnedd Llewelyn is to descend

Carnedd Llewelyn and Yr Elen from Yr Aryg

the east-south-east ridge to the cliffs of Craig yr Ysfa with its sudden dramatic view down a huge gorge known as The Amphitheatre. This is flanked on the left by sheer cliffs and on the right by the pinnacled ridge of Amphitheatre Buttress. A wide scree fan sweeps out of The Amphitheatre to the head of Cwm Eigiau more than a thousand feet below. The Amphitheatre is untypically rocky - as from the ridge the cliffs appear for the most part heavily vegetated though very steep.

The path continues down above the cliff in a series of tricky rock steps where extra care must be exercised especially in wet or icy conditions. However, these intricacies are short-lived and the col between Craig yr Ysfa and Pen yr Helgi-Du is reached. From here you may see walkers toiling up the steep shaly path from the shores of the Ffynnon Llugwy Reservoir, which is now reached by a Water Board road and offers a quick but dull descent to Helyg.

It is much more pleasurable to take the short steep ascent to Pen yr Helgi-Du by a steep path that threads between crags interspersed with bilberry and heather. Although a steadying hand is occasionally needed on this ascent, nowhere could the way be classified as hazardous. A path that traverses the mountain's western slopes marks the start of the steepest section and here is a good place to enjoy the scene across Ffynnon Llugwy towards Tryfan, whose profile from this viewpoint is wedge-like and stands proud of the loftier Glyders.

Pen yr Helgi-Du's summit is the culmination of a grassy whale-back ridge, Y Braich, which ends abruptly, its northern craggy slopes sweeping to the depths of Cwm Eigiau. At their foot lies an old quarry with the course of its tramway still discernible, a reminder of a bygone industry. How different must this now remote valley have seemed when the noises of man and machinery filled the air.

The descent is an easy one, following the gentle grassy spur of Y Braich to join the Bwlch Trimarchog route at the leat. Go through the gate, cross the bridge over the leat and descend to the A5 at Helyg and thence to Gwern-y-gof Isaf.

THE DOLGARROG HYDRO-ELECTRIC SCHEME

Those who opt for the low-level route will pass a complex system of leats, pipelines and reservoirs. These belong to the hydro-electric scheme originally devised to supply power to the aluminium works at Dolgarrog, utilising the tremendous energy available from the watercourses that flow from the Carneddau mountains. The scheme involved enlarging Llyn Cowlyd and constructing a new storage reservoir, Llyn Eigiau, but was short-lived as disaster struck soon after its completion.

On the evening of the 3rd November 1925 the powerful pressure of Eigiau's waters burst through the dam, flooding the wide upper valley of the Porth-llwyd before being channelled into the bottleneck of the Dolgarrog Gorge, high above the helpless village. Boulders weighing over two hundred tons were gouged from the mountainsides and thrust down with the raging torrents destroying cottages. A furnace at the aluminium works was flooded resulting in violent explosions.

Sixteen lives were lost that night. It is said that the death toll would have been greater but for the fact that many of the villagers were at the cinema, which is situated on higher ground and was not affected by the floods.

It was discovered, in retrospect, that the dam had been built on insecure ground (moraine debris) and had shifted under the immense pressure of the reservoir's headwater. The dam was never rebuilt and the contracted lake is now some 14ft lower than its previous level.

The aluminium works was closed but the power station continues as part of a redesigned scheme and by 1957 four generators were operational for the public supply of electricity.

The present system is served by both high and low-level water catchments. The high-level collects water from the Afon Dulyn and passes it by tunnel to Llyn Cowlyd via Llyn Eigiau. A 3 mile leat collects the waters of the Ffynnon Llugwy. In the low-level catchment, waters are collected from the Roe, Dulyn, Porth-llwyd and Ddu rivers and fed into the Coedty Reservoir. Pipelines (2m diameter reducing to 1.2m) convey the water down to the power station from both Coedty and Cowlyd Reservoir.

FACT FILE

Distances and Time

Low-level route via Cwm Eigiau	14mls	22km	8 hours
Mountain route	12mls	19km	9 hours
Foul weather route via Llyn Cowlyd	14mls	22km	9 hours

Terrain
High moorland plateaux on all routes

Accommodation
Hotels and B&Bs at Llanfairfechan, Capel Curig and Bethesda
Youth hostels at Rowen and Idwal Cottage (Ogwen Valley)
BMC bothy at Helyg (for members)
Campsite and bunkhouse at Gwern-y-gof Isaf, Helyg

Tourist Information
Llandudno Tel 01492 76413

CHAPTER 2
The Glyders and Snowdon
Helyg to Nantgwynant

Is a walk through High Wales complete without scaling its loftiest peak, Snowdon? For experienced backpackers looking for a high mountain challenge walk across the principality, the answer has to be no. I must stress, however, that as backpacking routes they are arduous; only the fittest could safely complete both Snowdon and the Glyders within one day and clear conditions would be advisable.

Those who are already familiar with these mountains may well be searching for new scenery and our main route should fit the bill. The ascent to the Glyder ridge via Braich y Ddeugwm has often been written of in glowing terms, but I have seldom seen anybody use this route, from which the finest views of Tryfan's buttresses may be enjoyed. The way down to Pen-y-Gwryd and the trek along the lonely, unspoiled Siabod-Moelwyn ridge offer views of the Snowdon group; slowly and subtly changing, they capture the attention throughout.

The final section of the route is characterised by endless permutations of intricate bluffs, secluded tarns and reedy shallow pools, many unrecorded on the maps; a ridge with countless quiet corners that are ideal natural mountain campsites. My favourites are near the tarn on the summit of Y Cribau and by the south-western lake of the Llynnau'r Cwn (Dog Lakes) trio (GR 662486).

For convenience of staging I have included descents to Nantgwynant. Although hard won ascent is lost, it may be necessary to replenish supplies at the post office / general store, or inclement weather may make it expedient temporarily to abandon the high ground. The ridge walk connection between Llyn Edno (the exit point to Nantgwynant) and Llyn yr Adar (where the low-level campers and those who have followed the high mountain route regain the ridge) is included for the discriminating backpackers who decide to make camp in this high paradise.

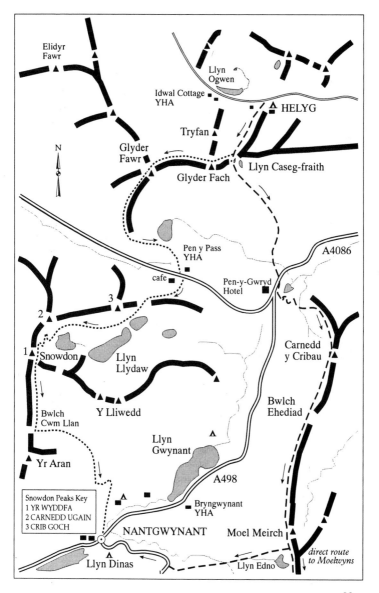

Snowdon Peaks Key
1 YR WYDDFA
2 CARNEDD UGAIN
3 CRIB GOCH

Elidyr Fawr

Llyn Ogwen

Idwal Cottage YHA

HELYG

Tryfan

Glyder Fawr

Glyder Fach

Llyn Caseg-fraith

Pen y Pass YHA

cafe

Pen-y-Gwryd Hotel

A4086

Snowdon

Llyn Llydaw

Carnedd y Cribau

Y Lliwedd

Bwlch Cwm Llan

Bwlch Ehediad

Llyn Gwynant

Yr Aran

A498

Bryngwynant YHA

NANTGWYNANT

Moel Meirch

direct route to Moelwyns

Llyn Dinas

Llyn Edno

HELYG TO NANTGWYNANT - The Main Route

Our route to the Glyder ridge begins at Gwern-y-gof Isaf (GR 685602) and climbs on a spur, Braich y Ddeugwm, which is only named on OS 1:25,000 maps. The best course is to keep to the crest of the spur except for the initial stretch, where a stile on its western side straddles an electric fence. The steep, grassy path rises amongst slabby crags and affords truly memorable views of Tryfan across its wild and little-frequented cwm. The gradient eases as Llyn Caseg-fraith is reached. A sketchy track passes through the marshy surrounds to the north of the lake and its tiny attendant pools. After rising to the head of Cwm Tryfan it meets the Miners' Track that links Ogwen and Pen-y-Gwryd. From here Glyder Fach's jagged northern spur, aptly named Bristly Ridge, vies for attention with Tryfan's magnificently sculpted buttresses in a view which also encompasses the Carneddau peaks and the snaking Holyhead road so far below.

The Miners' Track crosses a grassy plateau before descending the craggy upper southern slopes of Glyder Fach. The Nant Ddu (stream) is passed beneath a fine cascade. Much of the rock is now interspersed with heather, whose vivid purple summer mantle makes a brilliant foreground to the wide southern vista which includes Moel Siabod, Cnicht and the Moelwyns separated from the Snowdon Group by the curving Gwynant Valley. In one of Snowdon's finest facades Crib Goch, Yr Wyddfa, and Crib-y-ddysgl appear huddled, all displaying classical mountain form. Reddish hues that give rise to the name Crib Goch (red ridge) can be seen on the cliffs that tumble to the Pass of Llanberis.

As it nears the valley floor, the Miners' Track crosses a dry-stone wall which it follows to the Nantgwryd river and thence across an undulating field to meet the road just east of the Pen-y-Gwryd Hotel.

The PYG, as the inn is affectionately known, has for a century been a prominent centre for the exploration of the Welsh Mountains, as well as the planning of Himalayan and Alpine expeditions. Here John Hunt (now Lord Hunt) and his team, who in 1953 were the first to climb Everest, met to make the final preparations before departing for Nepal. On their reunion at the PYG they presented landlord and fellow climber Chris Briggs with a piece of summit rock which is still kept here. The Climbers' Bar has a ceiling which has been autographed by many climbers including the summit pair, Sir Edmund Hillary and Sherpa Tenzing. The inn offers good food including excellent quiches, salads and apple pie, and makes an ideal lunch stop.

Beyond the PYG the route once more ascends, this time to the Siabod/Moelwyn ridge. A second stile on the eastern side of the Beddgelert road (A498) allows entry to the marshy land north-west of Cefnycerrig, the rock-crested spur rising to the main ridge. Traverse the northern slopes of the small hill ahead and make a bee-line (south-east) for Cefnycerrig's lowest crags crossing the Nant-y-llys on the way. The track, marshy in places, then follows a fence to the ridge at Bwlch Rhiw'r Ychen (GR 676540 - not marked on 1:50,000 maps). Both sides of the pass are guarded by vegetated crags which overlook Llynau Diwaunedd, remotely situated beneath Moel Siabod's featureless south-facing slopes. Forestry Commission conifer plantations now surround three sides of the tarn, an intrusive incursion into the wild terrain.

From the bwlch, a path bordered by the ridge-fence twists amongst bilberry and boulders on a steep but short pull to the airy summit of Carnedd y Cribau. The succeeding ridge is punctuated by a series of delightful shallow tarns which provide interesting preliminaries to the steep fall to Bwlch Ehediad, a dull, grassy hollow preceding the rise to Moel Meirch. (NB: Youth hostellers bound for Bryngwynant should leave the ridge here using a path heading north-west.)

A narrow track ascends alongside the fence, hereabouts dilapidated, and heads towards the rocky crest of Moel Meirch. It passes through intricately-faulted and gnarled rock formations interspersed with deep heather. Just north of the summit are two boggy areas which can be avoided by keeping to the west side on heathered verges. A visit to Moel Meirch's very highest point will necessitate a slight detour and a short scramble westwards from the path at the head of Cwm Edno.

Llyn Edno's appearance is sudden. It will have been anticipated for quite a while but frequent rocky knolls have marred all previews. The trout-filled lake occupies a shallow stony basin south of Moel Meirch and is a favoured spot for anglers. Looking westwards beyond Llyn Edno, the view of Snowdon highlights the profile of that knife-edged ridge between Crib-y-ddysgl and Crib Goch, whose pinnacles are plainly visible. To their left is the pointed summit of Yr Wyddfa which dwarfs the Lliwedd peaks which are seen end on.

Descent to Nantgwynant

Walkers who have rejected the idea of a high-level camp can quit the ridge by following the Afon Llyn Edno as it descends to the Nanmore Lane. The river is very beautiful in its lower course where it bounds vigorously amongst rocky slopes lined with colourful rhododendron bushes. The path meets the lane beyond Hafodydd Brithion farm (GR 640494) just one mile short of Nantgwynant.

Ridge route via Ysgafell Wen and Llyn yr Adar

I have to recommend that in calm conditions a mountain camp be made. On this section of the ridge there are numerous secluded and sheltered sites where one can relax and watch the sun set behind the peaks of Snowdon. The path climbs south-east from Llyn Edno to Ysgafell Wen whose steep eastern brow overlooks the marshlands that are the source of the Afon Lledr. The heather of Moel Meirch has been replaced by more verdant hill pastures although the frequent rock outcrops remain.

A small reedy tarn, the most easterly of Llynnau'r Cwn (the Dog Lakes) is seen from the highest point of the ridge. A trackless south-westerly course from the eastern tarn will descend to Llyn yr Adar, another anglers' retreat, though they have competition from the hundreds of gulls who flock to the islet at the centre of the lake. The views of Snowdon from here are superior to those from Llyn Edno for the ridge obscures less of its lower slopes: much of the Watkin Path can be traced. Llyn yr Adar is not an ideal place for camping although the views are terrific. It is too exposed and its shores are a little too marshy for tents. The area around the Dog Lakes is much better.

On the north-eastern shores of Llyn yr Adar the path converges with the one that has ascended from Nantgwynant via Llyn Llagi (described in the next chapter).

THE HIGH MOUNTAIN ALTERNATIVE

From the head of Cwm Tryfan (GR 667583) the high mountain route takes a westerly direction on an increasingly rocky path to Glyder Fach's summit. Always prominent in the view ahead is the narrow jagged spur of Bristly Ridge descending steeply to Bwlch Tryfan.

Glyder Fach's bouldery summit plateau has noteworthy (and much photographed) features which include The Cantilever a large flat slab securely supported at one end by a group of vertical pillars, and Castle of the Winds (Castell y Gwynt), a huge serrated outcrop obstructing the way to Glyder Fawr beyond. The descent of Glyder Fach involves skirting around the southern side of the castle to gain Bwlch y Ddwy-Glyder situated high above Llyn Bochlwyd.

The way to Glyder Fawr is now gradual and easy going but confusing in misty conditions. In clear weather the views are magnificent. To the north, beyond the Nameless Cwm and Llyn Idwal, the gaze can wander to the rugged Pen yr Ole Wen and down the Nant Ffrancon to the Menai Straits and the flat plains of Anglesey. However, it is the great Snowdon massif to the south-west that commands most attention. The four peaks that surround the great glaciated hollow of Cwm Dyli form a distinctive skyline in which the classic Snowdon Horseshoe walk can easily be traced. Glyder Fawr's extensive top is not as rough as its smaller neighbour but is made interesting by frequent teeth-like rock protuberances.

The descent south from the summit is waymarked by red arrows painted on rocks assisting route-finding to Pen y Pass and leading walkers away from the complex cliffs of Llanberis Pass. Although intended to help with navigation, they have invoked considerable ire in some mountaineering circles. In my opinion these markings are fairly unobtrusive and a positive aid, in misty conditions, to a safe descent, though one wouldn't wish them to proliferate elsewhere.

In its lower reaches the path meanders through a more grassy terrain, although there is no shortage of boulders on which to daub the red arrows. As Yr Wyddfa sinks from view behind their ridge Crib-y-ddysgl and Crib Goch assume greater prominence in the scene across the valley. Llyn Cwm-y-ffynnon, a squarish-shaped lake in a shallow marshy hollow, is passed via its south-western shore before the short, steep descent to the Pen y Pass Youth Hostel

Castell y Gwynt (Castle of the Winds), Glyder Fach summit

which stands at the head of the wild Pass of Llanberis.

Across the road is the Gorphwysfa Restaurant, an ideal place to rest and dine before tackling Snowdon. (NB: At least $4^{1}/_{2}$ hours will be needed to complete the section to Nantgwynant.)

There are two alternative direct routes to Snowdon from here - the Miners' Track and the Pig (frequently misnamed PYG) Track. The former is a good path that skirts the lakes of Teyrn, Llydaw and Glaslyn in the cradle of Cwm Dyli before climbing the zig-zags to Bwlch Glas and thence to the summit. This popular track passes close to the derelict copper mines. The Pig Track climbs westwards out of the Llanberis Pass to Bwlch y Moch (Pass of the Pigs) before entering Cwm Dyli. Its course fits more naturally with its mountain surroundings with a greater variety of views and is thus chosen as the primary route.

A signpost guides the walker to the path which scales the northern slopes of the hill known as the Last Nail in the Horseshoe. Crib Goch is always prominent, towering above the Llanberis Pass. Glyder Fawr's south-western crags, particularly the last outlier, Esgair Felen, increasingly vie for attention as Bwlch y Moch is neared.

Bwlch y Moch provides a natural stopping place to savour the grandeur of the scene around Cwm Dyli, where the expansive, blue-green waters of Llyn Llydaw lie far below. The Miners' Track can be seen crossing the lake via a causeway that can be submerged after prolonged periods of rain. Beyond Llyn Llydaw vertical cliffs rise to the twin summits of Y Lliwedd. Yr Wyddfa at the head of the cwm is visible over the shoulder of Crib Goch, where the path divides. One way ascends directly to Crib Goch and the other, which is the Pig Track, traverses its southern slopes.

As the well-trodden path rises gradually across Crib Goch's slopes it provides a viewpoint from which it is possible to see, high above on the northern skyline, climbers tentatively scaling the pinnacles of Crib Goch.

After about a mile a spur is crossed and Glaslyn is revealed beyond. The path veers north-north-west above the outfall of the deep green lake which is tightly encircled by the precipitous dark cliffs and screes of Yr Wyddfa and Crib-y-ddysgl. The lake was once believed to have been bottomless and is the subject of a legend involving a damsel and a monster. The nearby cliffs of Y Lliwedd and Bwlchysaethau are also linked to legend. The Miners' Track climbs from the shores of the lake to meet our route which now begins its spectacular ascent out of Cwm Dyli via the zig-zags. (If time is pressing the route can be shortened at this point by taking the Y Gribin ridge that links the eastern end of Glaslyn with Bwlchysaethau. This is a stiff scramble, comparable to Crib Goch or the Bristly Ridge, but it does allow the Watkin Path to be reached without an arduous climb over Yr Wyddfa.) The section of the path that leads up to the crest of the ridge above has been so scarred and eroded by storms and walkers that it has attracted the attention of the path improvers. A painted metal sign, which would not look out of place in a Manchester subway, directs the walker along a blatantly obvious rock-slabbed stairway that gains the height in one large zig, thus avoiding the previous eroded slopes. This unnatural intrusion into such a wild scene is jarring and will probably take many years to blend acceptably with its surroundings.

A huge monolith marks the exit of the track at Bwlch Glas, the pass between Snowdon's two highest summits. This makes a junction with the long walking route from Llanberis and the Snowdon Mountain Railway. There now remains a short easy ascent following the line of crags at Cwm Dyli's edge. Vistas of Cwm Dyli are seen at their best from the ridge halfway between the bwlch and Yr Wyddfa's summit. From here Llyn Llydaw and Glaslyn can be seen in their entirety surrounded by the ridges of Lliwedd, Crib-y-ddysgl and Crib Goch which together with Yr Wyddfa comprise the Snowdon Horseshoe. The razor-like edge of Crib Goch's pinnacles can be appreciated standing out boldly in front of the more distant panorama of the Glyders and Moel Siabod.

The flat-roofed monstrosity of Snowdon's 'hotel' and railway terminus is hated by all when closed and used by most when open. I for one do not begrudge the king's ransom demanded at the bar for a can of lager when I have toiled long on a hot summer's day.

For all its commerciality the summit of Snowdon offers the finest vistas in all Wales. To the west beyond the Nant y Betws and Llyn Cwellyn is Mynydd Mawr where smooth grassy slopes terminate abruptly at the shattered Craig y bera whose broken crags disintegrate into immense screes. In the foreground the dark cliffs of Llechog command a cwm housing three shallow tarns. The view northwards is dominated by the railway gradually descending the grassy escarpment to Llanberis. In the southern panorama, Cnicht and the Moelwyns lead the eye to the more distant and hazy mountains of the Harlech Dome and Cadair Idris.

A narrow ridge declining south-west to Bwlch Main and thence southwards is used on the descent from Snowdon's summit. This descent is dramatised by views to the left where the severe cliffs of Clogwyn Du plunge over 2,000ft to Cwm y llan, a gigantic hollow enclosed by the stony flanks of Lliwedd and Yr Aran to the south. At the cwm's verdant base lie the ruins of the South Snowdon Slate Works.

After a slight ascent to a subsidiary top known as The Saddle, the route heads towards Bwlch Cwm Llan (GR 605523) (not marked on 1:50,000 maps). At the bwlch, distinguished by a small tarn and quarry, the route descends eastwards on Yr Aran's grassy slopes to join the firm track of a dismantled tramway, south of the great cliff of Craig-ddu. It meets the popular Watkin Path near to the stone ruins of Plas Cwm Llan. I have often seen tents pitched here and it

Snowdon's south ridge seen from Yr Aran

looks a good site, being next to the river.

As the arms of Lliwedd and Yr Aran close around the brim of the cwm, the river vigorously comes to life thundering down in a series of cataracts and a very impressive waterfall to the plains of Nantgwynant.

The barren mountainsides now wear a new verdant mantle. 'Real' trees, not the blanket of tedious spruce but small copses, line the slopes accentuating their majestic form. The path that winds into Nantgwynant is a solidly constructed one, and as 'improved' paths go is reasonably tasteful. The view of the mountains to the south are to the craggy Moelwyn range and Cnicht, with its well-spaced twin summit bluffs.

After passing the pleasant Parc Hafod-y-llan woods, which are lined with rhododendron, a lane leads to the Beddgelert-Capel Curig road at Pont Bethania.

For those who are to stay the night in the valley there is a campsite at Llyndy-isaf farm (GR 626498); the Bryngwynant Youth Hostel is one mile away on the Capel Curig road, and the hotels of Beddgelert are a little less than four miles south-west. (This is best reached by a beautiful walk south of Llyn Dinas and the Afon Glaslyn.) Those preferring a mountain camp might well press on to Llyn Llagi (GR 650483), a beautiful tarn situated beneath huge dark cliffs that rise to the Moelwyn ridge.

FACT FILE

Distances and Time

Low-level route to Nantgwynant	11mls	18km	7 hours
Mountain route	13mls	20km	10 hours

Terrain
Rugged mountain paths and boulder slopes on high route; some hard pulls on mainly grassy slopes on low route

Accommodation
Hotel at Pen-y-Gwryd
Youth hostels at Pen y Pass and Nantgwynant
Campsites at Nantgwynant

Tourist Information
Beddgelert Tel 01766 86 293

The beach at Llanfairfechan at the start of the walk (Chapter 1)

Bwlch Trimarchog, the final pass on the first low-level section before descending to the Ogwen Valley (Chapter 1)

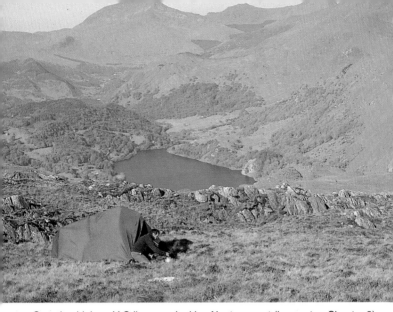

Camping high on Y Cribau overlooking Nantgwynant (low route - Chapter 2)
Llyn Llydaw from the summit of Snowdon (high route - Chapter 2)

CHAPTER 3

Over the Moelwyn Ridges
Nantgwynant to Trawsfynydd

Those who camped on high will, with a little luck, be blessed with clear morning sunlight embellishing the crags and cwms of Snowdon and glinting on the waters of a Moelwyn tarn. They will eat their bacon and eggs with the comforting knowledge that most of the day's toils have been avoided by not making the descent to Nantgwynant on the previous afternoon.

Provided that they were not over-indulgent at a Beddgelert alehouse, those who did make that descent will enjoy superb scenery to recompense the extra effort involved in the reascent of the Moelwyn ridge. Especially memorable are the retrospective views of Snowdon and the dark broken cliffs that tower above the high and lonely tarn, Llyn Llagi.

The northern Moelwyn ridge is unspoilt but there is stark contrast at Bwlch y Rhosydd to the east of Cnicht. Here, at the derelict Rhosydd Quarries, the mountainsides have been cut and scarred revealing their blue Ordovician core; but for all their ugliness, the ravages and relics of these old workings arouse immense interest and curiosity in the traveller. The steely colours of the mountains are transformed to green as the route descends through beautiful oakwoods into the Vale of Ffestiniog and twists and turns amid the undulating country into Trawsfynydd.

NANTGWYNANT TO TRAWSFYNYDD - The Main Route

A narrow, winding lane leaves the A498 at Nantgwynant (GR 626503) and climbs in a general south-easterly direction towards the Moelwyn ridge. Opposite the converted chapel of Blaen Nant (GR 635490) a path heads east, descending to cross a small stream with a farm building on the right. Delightfully situated amongst oak and rhododendron, the white-washed farmhouse, Llwynyrhwch, is passed to the north. From here a well-defined track winds through

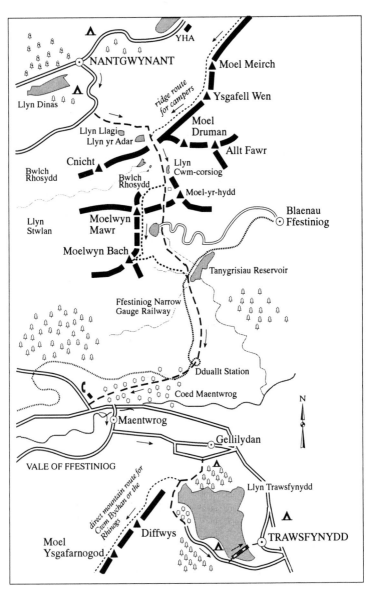

a complex but beautiful landscape of pasture, dry-stone walls, foaming cataracts and busy streams flowing through broad-leafed copses: and always standing proud in the view ahead - the broken, heather-clad crags of Ysgafell Wen and Moel Meirch.

The land is more marshy as the path approaches Llyn Llagi, a circular tarn completely overshadowed by the sombre vertical cliffs that tower from its eastern edge. The expanse of rock is briefly interrupted by a cascade which is fed by the waters of Llyn yr Adar 600ft above.

A well-cairned track rises eastwards to avoid the precipices. Just beyond a stream crossing, at a point marked by a large cairn, the track turns to the south rising on a bouldery course to the ridge before veering south-west to reach the shores of Llyn yr Adar. This is circumvented on its east side through marshy grassland to the col between Ysgafell Wen and Cnicht (GR 657477). This latter peak is best viewed from the south-west from where it is seen as a Matterhorn in miniature. Its profile is less arresting from the east but it can easily be climbed.

A well worn south-west bound path leads to the summit, a worthwhile diversion for strong walkers who will be able to make up the extra hour required. Their efforts will be rewarded with wide panoramas across Tremadog Bay and the Rhinogs, unrestricted views of Snowdon's southern face and an interesting angle on Moelwyn Mawr, which displays the scars of defunct quarrying activities. The main route, however, descends south-eastwards in a series of rocky shelves at the head of Cwm-y-foel, whose shapely lake beneath the screes of Cnicht lies precariously close to the edge of the cavernous Cwm Croesor.

After passing the small reservoir of Cwm-corsiog the path descends further to Bwlch y Rhosydd, a high pass between Cwm Croesor and Cwmorthin. Here, just 60 years after the closure of the huge slate quarries and mines, the buildings lie dilapidated, crumbling into the surrounding slag heaps. The blue-grey scars slowly heal beneath mossy and lichenous scabs as the quarry is slowly masked by nature. As I write there are plans afoot to recommence quarrying here; I hope they are resisted but fear they will not be. New roads may well make map-reading more complex.

Behind the quarry buildings, colossal spoil heaps litter the swelling slopes of Moel-yr-hydd and Moelwyn Mawr whose grassy apexes just rise above the ravages of industry. In a peaty hollow between the peaks, amongst further slate workings, lie two cavernous collapsed mine chambers.

The industrial relics have their uses however and an old tramway behind the main quarry building provides a route out of Bwlch y Rhosydd (not marked on 1:50,000). The path passes east of one of the spoil heaps and quarry pits before reaching the depression between Moel-yr-hydd and Moelwyn Mawr. At just over 1,800ft this is the highest point of the main route in the southern Moelwyns and from here a descent must be made to the Vale of Ffestiniog. The descent commences in a southerly direction across splintered slaggy slopes followed by a wet grassy course above the cliffs of Ceseiliau Moelwyn.

At the cliff's edge we are confronted by the Stwlan Reservoir, man's most savage affront to the Moelwyn's dignity. This reservoir and the larger Tanygrisiau Reservoir, seen still further down the eastern mountainside, are part of the Ffestiniog Power Station and Pumped Storage Scheme. The concrete monstrosities of dam and intake gates are totally alien to an otherwise magnificent scene.

From the sterile lake-shores rises the majestic slope of Moelwyn. Moelwyn Bach at its far side is characterised by a profile that resembles a human face. The quartz-veined rock facade of the ridge, Craigysgafn rises to its zenith at the domed summit of Moelwyn Mawr.

The descent to Llyn Stwlan skirts the precipitous crags on its north-west shore and care must be exercised as there are one or two tricky parts. A tarmac lane is encountered at the northern end of the dam and this is used until it reaches the Afon Stwlan at the dam's other edge. After crossing the stream a path leads south-eastwards to the huge Tanygrisiau Reservoir.

For much of the way the path traces the course of an old stone wall. It then meets the Nant Ddu, a lively stream which is crossed using a footbridge set amongst trees and a ruin. From here continue to the southern tip of the lake beyond which the Ffestiniog narrow gauge railway is crossed. An unsurfaced lane leads southwards joining the old course of the railway (now dismantled) north of Dduallt Station, whose platform constitutes part of the route. The path crosses the railway track just south of the station and heads south-west across grassy slopes before descending to and recrossing the line to the east of Dduallt farm. The way continues down through a splendid oak wood - Coed Maentwrog, now a designated nature reserve, and emerges above the lovely Vale of Ffestiniog where the Afon Dwyryd lazily meanders through its wide, green-pastured valley.

On leaving the oakwoods the path meets the B4410 near to the Oakley Arms (GR 659409). The charming village of Maentwrog is reached by following this road past the hotel, turning left along the A487 and then crossing the old three-arched bridge, which carries the A496 over the Afon Dwyryd.

Maentwrog, situated in a quiet corner of the Vale of Ffestiniog, consists of a cluster of grey stone, slate-roofed dwellings shaded by the steep afforested slopes of the Harlech Dome's foothills.

Its name means the stone of Twrog. Twrog was a seventh century Celtic Christian and giant who was said to have hurled the sandstone pillar from the mountain above the village to the churchyard where it still stands. A more practical theory is that the stone was placed by the Romans to mark the intersection of two of their roads.

A country lane (starting at GR 665405) rises out of Maentwrog revealing excellent views of Moelwyn Bach's rugged southern face. If a right turn is made at the first junction and a left at the second this will lead to Bryntirion farm (GR 680392) from where a track leads southwards to conifer plantations. The path converges with one from the Trawsfynydd Power Station before passing behind its reservoir's northern dam.

Across the vast waters of Llyn Trawsfynydd the moorlands of the Migneint swell to the twin-peaked summit of Arenig Fawr. Much closer are the splintered knolls that rise to form the northern Rhinogs, which look like mountains stolen from a western movie set. The path, sketchy on this section, skirts the lake's shores over a leat, then through a field of bracken before joining a well-defined track above the oak copse of Coed y Rhygen. It then climbs to the shoulder of a rocky spur, Craig y Gwynt, which offers the best view of the lake, with the Moelwyns (Moelwyn Bach dominant), the Migneint, Arenig Fawr and Aran Fawddwy forming the east and northern horizons. For those who are opposed to nuclear power,

Moelwyn Bach seen from Moelwyn Mawr

and I number myself amongst them, the sight of the Trawsfynydd Station, set intrusively amongst attractive woodland, tempers the scene with a silent and invisible menace which was sometimes accentuated by steam rising from the warm waters of the lake.

The early magnox type station was completed in 1965 but, thankfully, is now being decommissioned after a lifetime dogged with unreliability. Originally rated at 500 megawatts it was soon reduced to 300 to reduce the effects of corrosion in and around the reactor core. The safety record deteriorated and there were many scares. These included a serious fire and minor incidents such as accidental emissions of radioactive carbon dioxide and leaking safety valves.

Much of the reason for concern over the station was that its inland siting and the use for a small lake for cooling did not allow the satisfactory dispersal of liquid radioactive wastes; long-lived isotopes such as Plutonium and Americium were detected in mud samples taken from the lake.

The path joins a narrow metalled lane on descending from Graig y Gwynt. (Note the footpath sign at GR 684358 - this is the one you will need to take to do the full Rhinog Ridge tomorrow - see alternative at the end of the next chapter.) A left turn at the junction a mile further on will lead to the southern dam from where a long narrow footbridge crosses the reservoir to reach Trawsfynydd village.

NB: If camping on the mountains turn right at the junction and refer to the next chapter.

THE HIGH MOUNTAIN ALTERNATIVE

A route linking the peaks of Moelwyn Mawr and Bach involves an extra 1,100ft of ascent and would be a worthwhile exercise in clear conditions. It gains vantage points aloof from industrial incursions where the mountain reigns supreme.

The mountain alternative diverges from the main route by the Rhosydd Quarry buildings (GR 665463) where it passes to the west of the huge spoil heap to their rear and climbs south-westwards on grassy terrain to the northern shores of Llyn Croesor. The distinctive outlines of Cnicht are always prominent in views to the west. A dam/causeway on the small reservoir's western edge is crossed before climbing southwards on a grassy spur to Moelwyn Mawr's summit, which is crowned with a stone trig point.

From the summit Snowdon, Moel Siabod, the Glyders, the Rhinogs and Cadair Idris can all be seen in distant panoramas, but the most impressive scene is that across the mountain's northern crags and scree to Cnicht, whose steep, scarred sides plunge to the depths of Cwm Croesor, 1,600ft below.

The easy southern grass slopes of Moelwyn Mawr are rudely interrupted by the rough ridge of Craigysgafn, and the descent to Bwlch Stwlan, the pass between the two Moelwyns, must be undertaken with care. Wide white veins of quartz are seen in the rocks. The view north-westwards from Bwlch Stwlan, a grassy col, encompasses the Stwlan Reservoir, the cliffs of Ceseiliau Moelwyn (popular with climbers) and the grey town of Blaenau Ffestiniog surrounded by dismal, slate-terraced mountainsides.

A narrow track from Bwlch Stwlan rises on the north-eastern face of Moelwyn Bach, traversing screes before rising south-westwards on a grass slope to the summit, an airy, isolated plateau of grass with outcrops of rock.

In unbroken southern panoramas, the skyline includes, in the east, the Berwyns and Arans, whilst the more westerly Cadair Idris leads the eye to the graceful arc of Cardigan Bay. Beyond the Vale of Ffestiniog by the northern reaches of the Harlech Dome is Llyn Trawsfynydd, with its nuclear power station on the western shore.

The route now described from the summit of Moelwyn Bach is not a recognised one and therefore there will be no evident tracks. Retrace your footsteps on the grassy eastern slopes until the prominent cliffs of Carreg Blaen-Llym come into view. An easterly course aiming for a point south of this feature will lead to the source of the Nant Ddu. Care will be needed in the initial stages when rocky shelves and knolls will have to be rounded. Follow the northern banks of the stream before crossing at the footbridge mentioned in the main route description (GR 676438) and then continue along the same paths to Trawsfynydd.

If the visibility is poor it would be wiser to retrace steps to Bwlch Stwlan, descend to Llyn Stwlan and make for the dam from which point the descent is described in the main route section.

FACT FILE

Distances and Time

Low-level route	16mls	26km	9 hours
Mountain route	15mls	25km	10 hours

Terrain
Ridge traverse with intermittent paths on both Moelwyn routes

Accommodation
Hotel and B&Bs at Maentwrog and Trawsfynydd; B&Bs at Gellilydan; campsite by eastern shores of Llyn Trawsfynydd. Youth hostels at Ffestiniog (off route)

Tourist Information
Beddgelert Tel 01766 66 293

CHAPTER 4
The Wild Rhinogs
Trawsfynydd to Barmouth

From the first steps out of Trawsfynydd village the magnetism of the Rhinogs is felt, hastening the march over the moorland which lies to their north-east and away from the power station and its polluted lake.

The range, which is more correctly known as the Harlech Dome and stretches twenty-two miles from Maentwrog to Barmouth, is particularly rugged and complex at its northern end, having the reputation of being the roughest terrain in Wales. It consists of thick beds of gritstone and shale formed in the Cambrian era. The much faulted rocks are riven by deep transverse canyons that create repeated obstacles to the hiker walking the 'ridge', and thus early roads, paths and tracks all ran east-west taking the natural lie of the land across the axis of the range. Boulders and scree from the eroded gritstone slabs are frequently covered with thigh-deep heather, making progress slow and treacherous. Craig Wion and all peaks to its north are extremes of this form and are, as such, particularly arduous for the backpacker.

Although dull by comparison, the section of the route I have chosen across the moorlands of Crawcwellt and the Coed-y-Brenin Forest offers a very quick passage to the big Rhinogs, leaving time and energy to complete the journey to Barmouth within a single day. I have listed a Northern Rhinog alternative but would stress that this would be a two-day route for experienced backpackers.

An ancient track, which threads through Bwlch Drws Ardudwy - a narrow, heathery ravine between the sombre crags of Rhinogs Fawr and Fach - facilitates the low-level route, which also follows the course of the old London to Harlech Mail Coach Road from the Ysgethin Valley to the Llawlech Ridge.

Despite the extremely rough going, those who follow the high-level route will be rewarded with superb views, good easy scrambling on Rhinog Fawr, and the circuit around the dramatically

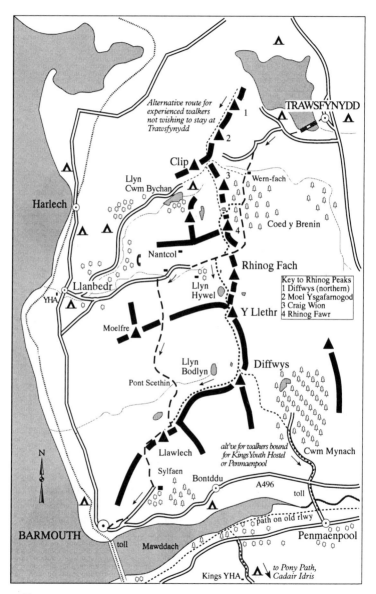

Alternative route for
experienced walkers
not wishing to stay at
Trawsfynydd

1

2

TRAWSFYNYDD

Clip

3

Wern-fach

Llyn
Cwm Bychan

4

Coed y Brenin

Harlech

Nantcol

Rhinog Fach

Llanbedr

YHA

Llyn
Hywel

Y Llethr

Key to Rhinog Peaks
1 Diffwys (northern)
2 Moel Ysgafarnogod
3 Craig Wion
4 Rhinog Fawr

Moelfre

Llyn
Bodlyn

Diffwys

Pont Scethin

alt've for walkers bound
for Kings Youth Hostel
or Penmaenpool

Cwm Mynach

N

Llawlech

Sylfaen

Bontddu

A496

toll

BARMOUTH

path on old rlwy

Penmaenpool

toll

Mawddach

Kings YHA

to Pony Path,
Cadair Idris

42

situated Llyn Hywel, surely the finest mountain tarn in Wales. Once past Y Llethr the rough terrain relents: the heather and boulders are replaced by smooth grassy ridges which allow rapid, carefree progress.

At the southern end new vistas unfold. The Mawddach Estuary, described by Wordsworth as 'sublime', is seen at its best around Llawlech, included in both high and low-level routes. Barmouth, the destination, lies on a narrow coastal strip beneath the fragmented cliffs of Garn, the last outpost of the Rhinogs. Here the smell of salt sea air mingles with the aroma from fish and chip shops and hamburger stalls.

TRAWSFYNYDD TO BARMOUTH - The Main Route

On leaving Trawsfynydd the route returns to the junction of minor roads near Tyndrain (GR 696347) at the southern end of the lake and follows the left fork for about a mile until a road sign (GR 687335) declares 'No footpaths beyond this point'. From here a south-west-bound cart track leads to the Afon Crawcwellt, which is crossed using a primitive slate-and-corrugated-iron footbridge leading to the recently refurbished cottage of Wern-fach from where the path heads up the grassy slopes of Moel y Gwartheg. The path is waymarked by yellow arrows on the fence-posts on the initial stages and later, as the path changes to a southerly course, on occasional rocks which become more abundant as altitude is gained.

The woods of Ffridd Maes-gwyn, part of the massive Coed y Brenin Plantations, lie directly ahead, whilst the oddly-profiled Craig Wion lures the gaze to the west. The forest is entered at a stile and more yellow arrows lead past a ruined stone building to a Forestry Commission road which is followed southwards. At GR 670299, just north of where the road crosses the Nant Llyn du, the high and low-level routes diverge. Those who opt for the latter choice continue to a left fork half a mile to the south and thence to another junction and a bend where a path leads west-south-west along the northern bank of the Afon Gau at the edge of the plantations.

The regimented ranks of larch and spruce give way to the tangled terrain of the lower Rhinog slopes. The way ahead is to Bwlch Drws Ardudwy, a rugged pass between Rhinogs Fawr and Fach, whose fissured crags rise from a rough seam of heather that is so typical of this range. The path is little more than a twelve-inch ribbon of compacted subsoil and rock through the thick heather, but it is always well defined making it impossible to stray from the route. The col is a wild place indeed. A rocky knoll rises from the base of the narrow gorge between the vying ramparts of the two Rhinog peaks and is marked with a large cairn.

From here the path descends Cwm Nantcol, where the wilderness is transformed into the green hues of cultivated land with the smoothly contoured Moelfre dominating the view ahead. The Cwm Nantcol road is joined at Maes-y-garnedd and this is followed until the public footpath sign beyond Cilcychwyn farm points the way southwards over the grassy eastern arm of Moelfre.

The path (also waymarked) is slightly to the east of the one shown on Ordnance Survey maps and rises to the col between Moelfre and Y Llethr. From the ridge it will be noticed that the valley of Ysgethin, to the south, is more barren and featureless than that of Cwm Nantcol. Two lakes, Llyn Bodlyn and Llyn Irddyn, lie beneath the sparsely-cragged, rounded hills of Diffwys and Llawlech respectively and the aura of this expansive, uninhabited valley is one of bleakness, making it easy to imagine the highway robberies that frequently took place in these parts. The ruins of an old inn, almost certainly frequented by the highwaymen, lie near to the small conifer copse at the southern foot of Moelfre. Here bandits once robbed a party of London gentlefolk who had halted at the inn on their way to attend a society wedding at Harlech.

The descent into the Ysgethin Valley is trackless but a bearing of 200 degrees (south-south-west) across rough grassland will lead to Pont Scethin, a small stone packhorse bridge which carried what was once the main highway between London and Harlech.

Beyond the well preserved little bridge a waymarked path zig-zags across marshy ground. It becomes quite a prominent grassy groove when raking acutely south-south-west up the steep slopes of Llawlech along the old London highway.

A little way up the hill lies Janet Haigh's Memorial Stone, which was erected by her son Melvyn, a Bishop of Winchester, after her death in 1953. It reads, 'To the enduring memory of Janet Haigh, who even as late as her eighty-fourth year despite dim sight and stiffened joints still loved to walk this way from Tal-y-Bont to Penmaenpool...Courage traveller'.

Pont Scethin, Rhinogs

The ancient road continues above the western crags of Llawlech, beneath which lies the lonely lake, Llyn Irddyn, a favourite spot of many Cambrian anglers. On reaching the ridge, the walker is rewarded with a fine prospect of the northern ramparts of Cadair Idris beyond the wide Mawddach Estuary.

The route now used follows the grassy ridge towards Barmouth, first rising to the summit of Llawlech and then descending to Bwlch y Rhiwgyr.

Bwlch y Rhiwgyr, or Pass of the Horns, got its name from the bandit watchmen who at nightfall would lie in wait for potential victims. They would sound their horns when the unwary traveller, perhaps a drover returning with moneys, passed, thus alerting a nearby band. A tale by William Davies (1898) tells of a man who knew of these bandits but, having faith in the speed of his horse, still decided to continue over the Bwlch at night. On reaching the top he saw the shadow of a horseman through the murk and heard the shrill sound of a horn. Suddenly he was surrounded. He decided to try and escape and made his horse go faster up the hill. The bandits gave up the chase and the man arrived home safely, but the following morning when he went to the stables he found the horse dead -

the effort had been too much.

It is possible to keep to the ridge beyond the Bwlch but the increasingly craggy hilltops are crossed by many high stone walls: progress over these will be slow and may cause damage to the environment. It is much better to descend the ancient drovers' route from the Bwlch to the whitewashed farm buildings of Sylfaen where a delightful country lane leads down to the sea at Barmouth.

THE HIGH MOUNTAIN ALTERNATIVE VIA COED Y BRENIN

The Rhinog mountain route is the toughest, roughest route in the book, and this is especially noticeable in the section north of Y Llethr. Here the hills know no gentle inclines but soar to the skyline in abrupt bluffs and buttresses often skirted by slippery screes and thick heather.

The divergence from the low-level is in the conifer plantations of Ffridd Maes gwyn by the Nant Llyn du. Instead of continuing along the forestry road, a right turn is made following a grassy path just north of the stream (GR 670299). A stile marks the exit from the woods and the first intimate prospect of the big Rhinog is unfolded.

The vertical slabs of Rhinog Fawr tower above to your left, while ahead is the tiny path through the thickly heathered slopes leading to Bwlch Tyddiad and the famous Roman Steps. The path to the Bwlch is followed until one leading southwards and directly towards Rhinog Fawr is reached (GR 661299). This rocky path leads to Llyn Du, a desolate spot over which Rhinog Fawr's northern face glowers unrelentingly. After traversing some slabs along the eastern shores of the lake the way ahead climbs steeply through a bouldered chute beneath a huge vertical wall of rock at the south - which involves some scrambling. This terminates on a heathery shelf with pleasant views of Gloywlyn and Carreg y Saeth. A path now climbs steeply to the left on scree-strewn upper slopes to reach the summit. The summit is marked by a cairn and a trig point and is adorned with a rich carpet of heather and bilberries, so different from the mountain slopes below. The view to the south is dominated by the huddled peaks of Rhinog Fach and Y Llethr whose craggy terraces cradle the high tarn of Llyn Hywel. To the north the eye can follow the horizon from the Lleyn Peninsula up a gradually rising mountain profile to Snowdon's five peaks. In an intimate north-western scene, two lakes, Llyn Cwm Bychan and Gloywlyn, nestle beneath the much faulted gritstone outcrops of Carreg-y-saeth and Clip respectively.

The scramble from Rhinog Fawr summit to Bwlch Drws Ardudwy is rough but not dangerous providing due care is exercised, particularly in the wet. There are many natural channels for the descent and although there are no obvious paths you will be on course if you keep approximately in line with Llyn Cwmhosan at the foot of Rhinog Fach. The Bwlch itself is usually quite boggy, especially by the wall that runs its length.

We are confronted by Rhinog Fach whose dark ramparts seem an obvious challenge, but one that I think should be ignored, for little is gained (views are inferior to those of Rhinog Fawr) and valuable time and energies are lost in its pursuit - especially as the alternative way is both logical and more dramatic.

A better course rises steadily, through the profuse heather, past the reedy shores of Llyn Cwmhosan and the huge boulders at the foot of the smaller Rhinog, and upwards until Llyn Hywel is reached. Of all the places on the walk, this is for me the most enchanting and the most memorable. On one side is Rhinog Fach, with its rocky crest overlooking loose bouldered slopes plunging to the lapping shores of the lake, whilst on the other is Y Llethr, displaying more greenery but ribbed with huge diagonal rock strata. The pattern is continued on the narrow connecting ridge where the gigantic slabs of Y Llethr rise out of Hywel's waters. Poor weather conditions render this vicinity wild and inhospitable but all the more impressive.

A way leads around the Rhinog side of Llyn Hywel and up to the ridge above, keeping left of the Y Llethr slabs on a path strewn with boulders. Those intent on climbing Rhinog Fach could possibly leave their heavy rucksacks here and scramble northwards up the bouldery wall-side path to its summit. The climb and the return journey would probably take about half an hour and make a pleasant diversion.

From the col above the slabs to the summit of Y Llethr the path is steep, but as there are marvellous retrospective views of the lake and Rhinog Fach there are plenty of excuses for frequent stops.

As Y Llethr's summit is reached the terrain changes. The contortions and rough going of the Rhinogs are quite suddenly replaced by very welcome, smooth, grassy ridges and the walking becomes easier correspondingly, so that the remaining section of the range to Barmouth is a genuine ridge walk.

From Y Llethr there is a large wall running along the ridge and this is followed on the western side. Our next peak is Diffwys and, providing the weather is reasonable, it should be clearly visible and easily reached on the connecting ridge, known as Crib y Rhiw.

To the left, nestling in some woods below, is a delightful lake, Llyn Cwm Mynach, with the heather-clad craggy peak of Y Garn forming the backdrop. The ridge now swells to Diffwys. The views from this peak are better than any in the range. The whole Cadair Idris group can be seen to great advantage across the Mawddach Estuary and there should be an uninterrupted view of the graceful curve of Cardigan Bay.

From Diffwys the ridge curves to the west, descending to a pass south of Pont Scethin, where the mountain route converges with the lower-level path on the descent to Barmouth.

An Alternative Descent from Diffwys to Penmaenpool

If time is short, or perhaps the weather turns nasty, the ridge can be left by the course of an old mine tramway which descends to these woods from the knoll just before Diffwys. A forestry road would then lead you to the A496 road to Pen-y-bryn. This would involve a major diversion from the described route via Barmouth. If this diversion is taken the best way to regain the main path would be to cross the Mawddach on the Penmaenpool Toll Bridge, then follow the course of the old railway and the lane that climbs through woodland past the Kings Youth Hostel to Ty Nant (GR 698152). Here the Pony Path can be used to Cadair Idris.

An Alternative Mountain Crossing from Llyn Trawsfynydd to Rhinog Fawr via the Northern Rhinogs

This is a very serious route and should not be undertaken by anyone not totally familiar with rough mountain terrain; only the fastest walkers will complete the Rhinogs this way in one day. It is however a fine route and shouldn't be dismissed by experienced walkers with a little extra time on their hands.

The route begins on the public footpath from the western shores of Llyn Trawsfynydd (GR 684358) and climbs to the ridge overlooking Cwm Moch. Now head southwards across very rough heather-clad terrain to the summit of Moel y Gyrafolen. There's a bit of a drop between this and the next peak Diffwys but the route, little more than sheeptracks on the ground, is entertaining with good views of the Lleyn Peninsula and the Arenig Mountains.

Foel Penolau's summit is guarded by tiered crags but is easily conquered - the first 2,000-footer of the day, presuming that you started at Trawsfynydd or Maentwrog. Its top is paved with massive slabs of gritstone and affords superb views back to the high Snowdonian giants. Snowdon and the Nantlle ridge are framed beautifully by the estuaries of Glaslyn and Dwyryd and the sky.

By descending Foel Penolau on its south-western flanks you can avoid scrambling on the more serious of its southern cliffs before continuing the short way to Moel Ysgafarnogod. This summit is easily recognised by its trig point and cairn. Head westwards from the summit to look down on the reedy horseshoe-shaped lake, Llyn Dywarchen, then descend southwards on a grassy arm. After straddling a rocky knoll you will come upon the dusky waters of Llyn Du, a splendid little tarn hemmed in by rock and scree. After tracing its eastern shores the route undulates on rocky knoll, over heather and over grass, to reach the shores of another tarn, Llyn Corn y Stwch, which is passed along its the north-western shores.

The route continues south-eastward above the Craig Ddwrwg and heather is largely replaced by rough grass. It is possible to make a short detour to Clip for its good views over Cwm Bychan but if time is short it would be more prudent to descend the boulder-strewn grassy channel of Bwlch Gwylim (not named on Landrangers, GR 654328) to the col between Clip and Craig Wion.

The next section is the most serious and the contours on the map cannot begin to prepare you for the real ups and downs. If you are tired why not drop down on the well-defined path to Cwm Bychan where there is a campsite; you could tackle the Rhinogs tomorrow, either by the Roman Steps route to the tops, or by the Gloywlyn route to join the low-level route at Nantcol. (NB: The path on the heather ridge above the lake is non-existent on the ground and good compass work would be necessary.)

If you are determined to go on, climb the ridge to Craig Wion where delightful lakes, Llyn Twr-glas and Llyn Pryfed, are firmly set amid slabs of rock and heather. Rhinog Fawr jumps in and out of view as you scramble in and out of dark ravines which traverse the route with tiresome regularity. At first the ridge runs south-eastwards; then it changes to south-west - the ravines just keep getting deeper. You stumble on Llyn Morwynion; follow the wall from its southern shores over a little summit. You may hear voices for the first time today, then you'll drop down to Bwlch Tyddiad and see the crowds who have come up the Roman Steps - maybe one or two of them will be doing Snowdonia to Gower on the main route from the Coed y Brenin Forest.

FACT FILE

Distances and Time

Low-level route	15mls	25km	9 hours
Mountain route to Barmouth	16mls	25km	12 hours
Mountain route to Kings YH	17mls	27km	13 hours

Terrain

High-level is rough terrain of heather rock and boulder. Low-level route minimises this and goes for routes through the passes

Accommodation

Hotel and B&Bs at Barmouth; Campsite at Barmouth. Those wanting intermediate accommodation are served by a campsite at Cwm Bychan and off-route hotels, B&Bs and campsites at Llanbedr and Dyffryn Arduddwy. Telephone for taxi at GR 623262. Off-route youth hostel at Llanbedr.

For those who quit the ridge at Diffwys there is a youth hostel at Kings and a hotel (expensive) at Penmaenpool.

Tourist Information

Barmouth Tel 01341 280787

CHAPTER 5

Cadair Idris and the Tarrens
Barmouth to Machynlleth

Whether you climb to its lofty summit or skirt its perimeters the massif of Cadair Idris will totally capture the centre stage of this section. In views from Barmouth's long bridge her proud precipices tower boldly above the wooded foothills that rise from the sands of the Mawddach Estuary, luring the walker in an irresistible challenge to set foot on her slopes.

The high route explores Cadair's craggy cwms and gullies, passing through a mountainscape as magnificently sculpted as any in Wales. A different side to the mountain's character is revealed on the lower route, when the gentle green slopes fall in graceful arcs to the valley of the Afon Cadair. Those who seek peaceful, secluded scenery will be in their element in this quiet corner of Cambria.

Beyond the slate-mining village of Abergynolwyn lie the little-frequented Tarren Hills which, although ravaged by extensive conifer planting, still retain their intrinsic wildness. These are the last outposts of the Snowdonia National Park, but they mark the beginnings of a new phase of the journey - that of the Elenydd or Green Desert.

BARMOUTH TO MACHYNLLETH - The Low-level Route

An exhilarating start to the day is provided by the walk across the Barmouth toll-bridge which commands extensive views along the Mawddach Estuary to the hills of Cadair Idris and Diffwys.

The $1/2$ mile-long viaduct, built in 1860 by the Welsh Coast Railway Company, is constructed from wood except for the part which spans the river's main Channel. Here a 400ft steel section, part of which swings open to allow the passage of ships, is supported by huge cylinders which were driven 120ft through alluvial deposits to penetrate the firm rock below. One side of the bridge carries the Cambrian Coast Railway linking Aberystwyth and Pwllheli and the other a delightfully convenient footbridge.

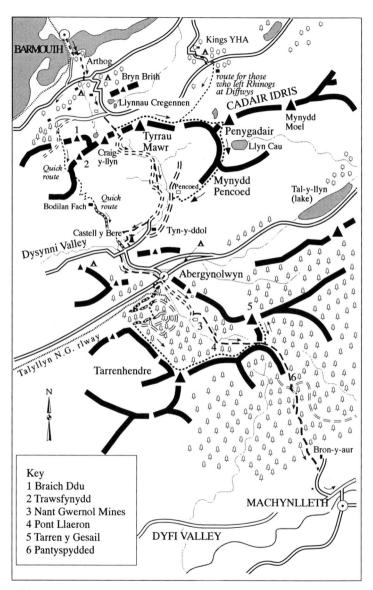

Key
1 Braich Ddu
2 Trawsfynydd
3 Nant Gwernol Mines
4 Pont Llaeron
5 Tarren y Gesail
6 Pantyspydded

On crossing the estuary, a footpath leads eastwards at the river's edge and skirts the wooded slopes of the diminutive knoll of Fegla Fawr. After passing to the south of a small group of terraced cottages, our route diverges from the riverside walk at GR 633149 and heads south-east, passing some allotments and a disused railway line, to the A493 road and Arthog just to the east.

From Arthog follow a lane signposted 'Cregennen Lakes'. This gated little lane winds its way up the western foothills of Cadair Idris and provides wonderful views across the Mawddach Estuary to Barmouth, before levelling out on reaching the shores of Llynnau Cregennen. The two small lakes are dominated by the cliffs of the northern face of Tyrrau Mawr.

A road junction is encountered just beyond the lakes and, after a short walk, a track heading into the mountains is located opposite a ruined farmstead, Hafotty-fach. After crossing two stiles, steep grassy slopes must be climbed to reach a pass at the lowest point of the ridge west of the summit of Tyrrau Mawr. This too is a splendid viewpoint. In the foreground, but far below, lie the two lakes of Cregennen, nestling beneath Bryn Brith's bold, rocky flanks. Across the Mawddach the descending ridge from Diffwys to the sea leads the eye to Barmouth, its far-reaching sand bars, and the long bridge spanning the estuary.

Just beyond the electric fence which runs along the ridge top and is scaled by a wooden stile, a right turn is made along a newly-constructed farm road which descends into the green valley of the Afon Cadair which has a surprisingly pastoral character that barely hints at its proximity to the craggy higher cwms of the Cadair massif less than 2 miles to the east.

The flinted track descends to Gwastadfryn farm where there is a delightful campsite next to the sprightly, tree-lined river. A small detour over the Cadair Bridge at Pennant farm (GR 673096) (unnamed on the 1:50,000 map) will enable you to see the ruins of Tyn-y-ddol.

Here stands a monument to a poor girl, Mary Jones, who walked 25 miles barefoot to the home of Thomas Charles at Bala in order to purchase a copy of the Bible - an act that is reputed to have inspired the formation of the British and Foreign Bible Society.

Beyond Pennant farm the route keeps to the Afon Cadair's

northern bank until it crosses at the footbridge near Maes-y-llan farm (GR 666091) and heads south across fields towards the western edge of a rock outcrop on which the fortress Castell y Bere is perched.

From here Prince Llewelyn-ap-Gruffydd stoutly resisted the armies of Edward I until, in 1283, he was finally defeated.

In the Dysynni Valley, a curiously-profiled rocky protuberance, Craig yr Aderyn (Bird Rock) juts out from the gentle, verdant neighbouring hills. The crag's upper section is a breeding ground for cormorants, one of the very few inland sites in the British Isles. The steep lower facet, close to the road, boasts a plethora of very difficult rock climbs.

The path meets a narrow country lane west of Llanfihangel-y-pennant. At this point the best course is to follow the lane south-westwards to the farm of Rhiwlas (GR 660078) by Pont Ystumanner.

From Rhiwlas a lovely path heads back south-east above the Afon Dysynni where it cuts through a narrow valley between Gamallt and Foel Cae'rberllan. Abergynolwyn is strategically placed where the valley opens out. The village, which originally relied on the quarrying activities, now thrives on the tourism brought by the Talyllyn narrow gauge railway, and on work provided by the Forestry Commission whose plantations cloak the slopes of the Tarren mountains to the south. It's the Tarren mountains that bar the way to Machynlleth.

The expanding clutches of the monotonous conifer forests are all too evident in the valley of the Nant Gwernol that leads south-east from Abergynolwyn, threatening to submerge even the 2,000ft hills of Tarrenhendre and Tarren y Gesail.

Nant Gwernol, which is also known as The Wild Ravine, is entered from Pandy Square, opposite the Railway Inn where a metalled lane rises up the south-west slopes of Foel-y-Pandy (unnamed on the 1:50,000 map) passing Hendrewallog farm before reaching the area of disused mines and quarries at Bryn-Eglwys. Many relics of the bygone quarrying industry are seen here, in an area devastated by slag heaps and mine shafts. (These shafts are in particularly poor condition and exploring their depths is not recommended.)

After passing close to a huge quarry pit on the left, a signed footpath (GR 694056) (not marked on the 1:50,000 map) leads off the track north-eastwards through sprucewoods. About 50yds further on it resumes its south-easterly course past the pulley house above the Beudnewydd Incline. (On these inclines pulley-driven trucks would carry slate from the mines to the valley floor.) A collapsed chamber can be seen to the west and into its murky recesses tumble two streams forming 50ft waterfalls.

Beyond the incline the well-defined grassy path, which can be marshy in places, rises above the old reservoir, now dry due to its dam being breached. Nant Gwernol turns to the east below the slopes of Foel y Geifr and is crossed using the ancient packhorse bridge, Pont Llaeron, said to be of Roman origin. Its wonderful situation has been savaged by the unsympathetic spruce plantations which now smother the surrounding slopes. Beyond the bridge, our path veers left at the edge of the plantations and parallel with the stream. After briefly entering the woods it emerges at a stile on the pass between Tarren y Gesail, the tallest of the Tarren range, and the summit of Foel y Geifr (GR 719056).

From here the path descends north-eastwards, with the ruins of old quarry workings directly ahead. After about 100yds take the right fork, which is little more than a sheeptrack. It joins the perimeter of plantations to the right and overlooks the edge of the thickly afforested chasm of Nant Lliwdy. A stile and gate to the right lead us into the forest on a track which descends southwards along the edge of Nant Lliwdy.

Yellow arrows intended to mark the course of the Dyfi Valley Way help to locate the line of the old path which diverts from the old forestry track in several places. After reaching the ruins of Pantyspydded (GR 728041) another waymark highlights the route which descends southwards on a less prominent forestry track (not shown on the 1:50,000 maps but represented for a short way by the red dotted lines of a footpath).

At GR 729033 there is a meeting of five forestry tracks. Snowdonia to Gower takes the one continuing in roughly the same direction but offset slightly to the left. This track soon establishes itself as a fine grassy road leading south-eastwards to the plantation's edge to the east of spot height 225m. The green road that follows is a joy to descend, with airy views of the hills of Maesglase, Mynydd y

Cyfrwy and Llyn y Gadair, Cadair Idris

Cemais and Pumlumon (Plynlimon) beyond the brilliant green fields of the Dyfi Valley. The track, tree-lined in the lower stages, meets a narrow tarmac lane by a house, Cwm-glia (GR 736023 - not marked on 1:50,000 map), and this leads to the A493 at Penrhyn Dyfi, just west of the Dyfi Bridge, which marks the southern boundary of Snowdonia National Park. Half a mile to the south lies the busy little market town of Machynlleth dominated by its ornate Victorian clock-tower, the focal point of this section of the route - the heart of Mid Wales.

THE HIGH MOUNTAIN ALTERNATIVE ON CADAIR IDRIS

In terms of mountain architecture, Cadair Idris's majesty is second only to Snowdon's and the high-level traverse of its peaks has to rank as one of the highlights of this long walk. If it is undertaken, only the very fittest will be able to traverse the mountain, cross the Tarren's mountain route and reach Machynlleth in one day and it would therefore be wise to plan a break at Abergynolwyn.

The mountain route breaks away from the low-level route on the ridge to the west of Tyrrau Mawr, which is the first summit visited

- the way guided by a fence running along the edge of the precipitous Craig-las cliffs. From the summit of Tyrrau Mawr views of the northern landscape are similar to those described from the pass above Hafotty-fach, although the mountains of Snowdonia are added to the scene. A glance to the east reveals the highest point of Cadair Idris, beyond Cyfrwy. To the south the Afon Cadair descends beneath Mynydd Pencoed, threading its way between some lesser hills towards Llanfihangel. The landscape hereabouts is more akin to moorland than mountain but, within 2 miles, this character totally changes, the contrast greatly enhancing the appeal of this mountain traverse.

The route from Tyrrau Mawr to Penygadair is straightforward. It meets the Pony Path at Rhiw Gwredydd, where you will probably be joined by other travelling companions on a well-used track to the summit. This leaves the cliffs' edge beyond Rhiw Gwredydd and rises on the southern shoulder of Cyfrwy until just before the last stretch to the major peak, where the magnificent rock sculptures of its northern face are revealed. At its foot is the apple-shaped tarn Llyn y Gadair, which is also flanked by the rock crested scree slopes of Cyfrwy. It is from this cwm that the rough Fox's Path works its way up steep, scree-strewn slopes.

The bouldered summit of Penygadair commands excellent views of Snowdonia's skyline, with the Arans prominent to the north-east. To the south, beyond the rounded Tarrens, Pumlumon (Plynlimon) rises above its moorland satellites. There is a covered shelter just below the summit for those who are unlucky enough to encounter bad weather.

Our route from Penygadair now heads south-west, skirting above the immense precipices surrounding Llyn Cau. As it descends, the views of the fine cwm enclosing this tarn become more spectacular, especially at the top of Great Gully which splits the vertical cliffs of Craig-y-Cau. From the col the route ascends towards Craig-y-Cau (GR 710122) but veers south-westwards just short of its summit, following the ridge-fence of Mynydd Pencoed. It traces the edge of the crag-rimmed Cwm Amarch, which directs the gaze down to the gleaming lake of Tal-y-llyn in the Dysynni Valley, far below. On the opposite shores of the lake the diminutive, white-walled Ty'n-y-Cornel Hotel is dwarfed by the steep slopes of Graig

Goch beyond.

Further along the ridge from Cwm Amarch is the summit of Mynydd Pencoed. From there the grassy western flank is descended to the old Pencoed farmhouse where the path leads to a farm road which fords the Nant Pencoed. A quarter of a mile further south a path to the right of the farm road goes down to the Afon Cadair, which it crosses via a footbridge and converges with the main route just north of Gwastadfryn farm.

THE TARREN MOUNTAIN ALTERNATIVE - ABERGYNOLWYN TO MACHYNLLETH

The main peaks of the Tarren range can be climbed in a horseshoe route around Cwm Gwernol south of Abergynolwyn, linking up with the second stage of the low-level route late in the day. The mountain alternative is particularly arduous, the Tarren's slopes being steep-sided and grassy - the sort of terrain that really hurts the calf muscles. However these wild and lonely hills offer lovely views of Cadair Idris and the Dyfi Estuary.

From just west of Abergynolwyn a forestry road leaves the B4405 at GR 674068, passes Hendre farm, and crosses the Talyllyn Railway before entering the plantations. After a right turn (west) at the first junction of forestry roads, the large flinted road makes a 'U' turn as it gently climbs the slopes of Foel Fach. At GR 678065 an old dilapidated stone wall marks the inconspicuous start of an overgrown footpath, which doubles back to assume a south-westerly course. The path follows the wall, passing a ruined dwelling before veering left up a grassy tract. This widens about 100yds further on and meets a flinted forestry track, which is followed to the forest's edge, marked by a gate (GR 670058).

The next complex section is made more confusing than normal by the need to switch to a new map (135) to the north of Tarrenhendre and then, on its east, revert to the old one (124), for a short while. Constant changes in the extent of the plantation boundaries compound the problem.

The route now traces the edge of the plantations ascending north-eastwards on steep grassy slopes above Mynydd Pentre towards Tarren-fach (on the southern edge of map 124). Views to the left include Cadair Idris rising above the conifer-cloaked Graig

Abergynolwyn from the path in Nant Gwernol, the Tarren Hills

Goch. Ahead is Tarrenhendre, a rounded, grass-covered peak ending abruptly at the chiselled north-eastern crags above the forest line. The final ascent to this summit is steep but the airy situation and the magnificent succeeding ridge-walk make the efforts worthwhile. There is an abundant variety of grasses hereabouts, enhancing the gentle slopes with an attractive blend of subtle hues. The view to the south is now dominated by the meandering Dyfi as it widens amidst huge sandbanks to meet the sea. Across the estuary lie the flat peat bogs of Cors Fochno, now a nature reserve and habitat of many rare species of plant, insect and sea-bird. Further distant to the south-east, Pumlumon rises from the rolling hills south of Machynlleth.

From Tarrenhendre's summit the route now turns sharply to the east by a ridge which leads towards Foel y Geifr at the head of the Wild Ravine. At this stage, if you have time in hand, continue along the ridge until the pass between Foel y Geifr and Tarren y Gesail is reached and then ascend the latter peak on a grassy spur with crags to the right. Insect-eating sundew are amongst the interesting range of plants on this summit. Views down to Nant Iago and the precipitous crags guarding the exit into the Dysynni Valley are magnificent.

After the ascent of Tarren y Gesail retrace the route to the previously mentioned pass, where the main low-level route is joined on a descending track to Pantyspydded farm. If time is pressing, the ascent of Tarren y Gesail can be omitted and after descending the Foel y Geifr ridge the low-level route may be joined at GR 719055.

OTHER ROUTE VARIATIONS

If you want to make up some time or you don't fancy the walk on tarmac to Cregennen there is another way. Instead of turning left beyond the Barmouth Bridge go straight on past the old railway station to the main road. Turn left along the busy road, then right on a footpath by a row of cottages and by an old quarry. It climbs to an old track, which veers to the right beneath some woods and into a shallow valley which channels the view ahead to the sea. Watch out for the path which zig-zags up through the woods to the left and passes Cyfannedd Fawr farm to Ffordd Ddu (the Black Road) at the termination of the tarmac. Immediately opposite is a grassy ride in the spruce forest that now cloaks the northern fellsides. Climb the ride to reach a flinted track beneath the hill named Trawsfynydd.

For those who want to make it quickly down to Abergynolwyn turn right then follow the footpath raking along the western sides of Trawsfynydd to meet a track descending to the country lane at Bodilan Fach farm. From here you can follow the lanes to meet the main route at the bridge over the Dysynni (GR 660078).

Mountain lovers should turn left along the flinted track to a stile in the fence which gives access to Braich Ddu, the western outlier of the mighty Cadair Idris range. Simply follow the ridge fence and enjoy the views. In mist watch out for turns at the bottom of Braich Ddu's southern ridge and also at the fence intersection above the cliffs of Craig-y-llyn. This is a spectacular vantage point overlooking the lonely tarn of Llyn Cyri. The Cadair mountain route is met at the pass between Craig-y-llyn and Tyrrau Mawr.

FACT FILE

Distances and Time

Low-level route	17mls	28km	9 hrs
Mountain route to Abergynolwyn	14mls	23km	9 hrs
Mountain route; Abergynolwyn to Machynlleth	11mls	19km	7 hrs

Terrain

Well-defined mountain paths on Cadair Idris mountain route. Steep intermittent paths on grass to the Tarrens. A complex of mountain paths, tracks and forestry roads for the low-level route

Accommodation

Hotels, B&Bs and campsite at Machynlleth; B&B, bunkhouse and campsite at Abergynolwyn

Tourist Information

Machynlleth Tel 01654 702401

Old Parliament Buildings, Machynlleth

CHAPTER 6

Tackling the Great Desert
Machynlleth to the Wye Valley

With the great peaks of Snowdonia behind us new landscapes unfold - less dramatic perhaps, but the contrast is nonetheless pleasant and stimulating. The rounded, green Silurian hills are breached by a maze of valleys - narrow slivers of verdant pasture and hedgerow flanked by steep, thickly wooded slopes. In the initial stages the heads of many such vales are passed before the route rises to the subtle-hued, windswept peaks of Hyddgen and the Northern Elenydd. South of the majestic, scree-girt cliffs of Creigiau Bwlch Hyddgen the hills become bare and seem much loftier than the map suggests. We are now truly in the midst of a wild, remote area long since deserted by the rugged sheep farmers.

Pumlumon Fawr, often incorrectly referred to as Plynlimon, has been unfairly described as a 'sodden weariness'. Most guidebooks only include the ascent from Eisteddfa Gurig via the old mines, probably the dullest route available. Take no notice! Pumlumon is a noble mountain, the highest in Central Wales and certainly the best vantage point to see both the north and south of the country. Being the birthplace of three great rivers, the Severn, the Wye and the Rheidol, it has its marshy places, but none on our route from the north, which takes in the beautiful glaciated cwm where dark Ordovician crags encircle the secluded tarn, Llyn Llygad Rheidol.

The high route tackles Pen Pumlumon Arwystli before dropping into the Hafren (Severn) Forest where it heads southwards down the Wye Valley to Pant Mawr. I have also described a descent to Dyffryn Castell near Ponterwyd for those who could not arrange accommodation at Pant Mawr.

I have included a low-level alternative round the shores of Nant-y-moch for use in foul weather but surely in settled conditions the route to the top is preferable.

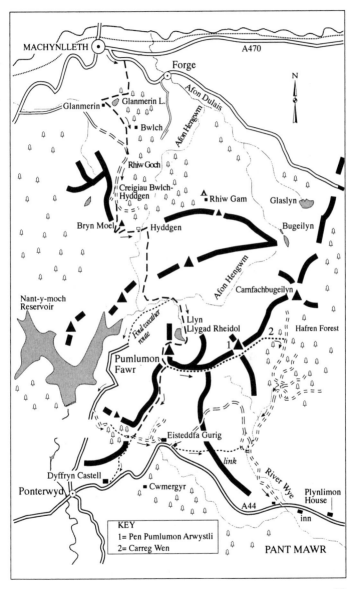

MACHYNLLETH TO PANT MAWR - The Main Route

From the busy streets of Machynlleth the Llyn Clywedog to Llanidloes mountain road leads south-eastwards towards the wild and desolate Elenydd Hills, sometimes known as the Green Desert.

At GR 754007 a signposted footpath crosses the town's golf course before zig-zagging up the steep, bracken-covered slopes of Parc from where impressive northern panoramas are revealed. Machynlleth, its clock tower protruding from the slate-grey roof-tops, is sheltered by a small, partially afforested hill. Beyond the emerald fields of the Dyfi Valley rise the pale Tarren Hills whose smooth contours are rudely distorted by the patchwork plantations of spruce and larch.

The Rheidol Forest is entered at GR 756995 and a signpost points the way to Glanmerin Lake. The route through the forest is short-lived and the path passes above the northern shores of the little lake before descending across crag-scattered slopes and scrubland to Glanmerin farm. A farm track heads south-eastwards above a pleasant little vale then climbs to a crossroads of routes at GR 752976 to the north of Bwlch farm. Hereabouts in spring the scene is transformed by brilliant splashes of colour added by the bluebells which grow in profusion.

Our route follows the track climbing south-eastwards to the west of Bwlch farm and passes a small copse before reaching the open fellsides high above Cwmyrhaiadr, a deep sylvan valley. Prominent in views to the south, Pistyll y Llyn, a spout-like cascade, tumbles 300ft down a crag-rimmed cwm.

Following a short descent, the route enters the Rhiw Goch plantations using a forestry road which heads south, close to Rhiw Goch's pointed summit. On leaving the forest on a stony track along the sharp north-east ridge, one of the walk's grand landscapes is presented. Amongst precipitous, dark, vegetated crags the Afon Hengwm plunges, a foaming torrent, into a huge, heavily afforested basin. Above the forest line on the cwm's western side are vast, sweeping screes, crested by the cliffs of Creigiau Bwlch-Hyddgen. On the southern skyline, beyond a coniferous sea, is Pumlumon whose fine northern aspect promises much. To the east its bare ochre foothills, divided by a complex system of glaciated valleys, are sparsely decorated with rocky cwms. There is a division of

Llynnau'r Cwn (the Dog Lakes), Moelwyn ridge (low route - Chapter 3)
Rhinog Fawr seen from Gloywlyn (high route - Chapter 4)

Overlooking Llyn Cau from the summit of Penygadair,
Cadair Idris (high route - Chapter 5)

Pont Llaeron in the Tarrens (low route - Chapter 5)

tracks at GR 765938. A right fork leads to Hafodwnog farm but the one used continues southwards on an undulating, grassy plateau above the cliffs at Creigiau Bwlch-Hyddgen.

It is difficult to imagine Bwlch-Hyddgen as anything other than a tranquil place far from the world's troubles but it was once the scene of a terrible battle - that of Nant Hyddgant (1401). On the slopes leading down to Hyddgen the English forces of Henry IV were slaughtered by those of Owain Glyndwr, Prince of Wales.

South-east of Foel fras at GR 768922 the track which enters the forest near Mynydd Bychan is quitted for a less distinct path which winds around Bryn Moel before a descent is made on a trackless course down its south-eastern slopes to the sheep-shearing sheds and ruins of Hyddgen, the scene of a tragic tale.

Locals often tell the story of a shepherd who was caught in a violent blizzard whilst working above Creigiau Bwlch-Hyddgen. After making strenuous efforts to return to his farm at Hyddgen he collapsed with fatigue. His wife was alerted when his work-horse returned alone. Fearing the worst she took a lamp, for it was now dark, and searched for her husband. Finding him unconscious, she attempted to drag him back to their home, but her supreme efforts proved unsuccessful and both died on that ferocious night.

It is said that at the end of the day a light can be seen wavering as it travels from the valley to the spot where the shepherd fell. The spot was marked by neighbours with a ring of white stones and, although most are scattered, those that remain can be seen from a nearby forestry road.

From the bridge over the Hengwm the mountain route continues south-east, then south along the western flank of Carn Hyddgen. At the foot of Pumlumon, the valleys of the Hyddgen and Hengwm meet and the eastern tip of the huge Nant-y-moch Reservoir comes into view. The Afon Hengwm (not the same river encountered at Cwm Hengwm) is crossed using a little concrete bridge to the east of the path. This is where the mountain route diverges from the foul weather route, choosing to strike for Pumlumon's highest top. If conditions are good the mountain route is the most rewarding.

HENGWM TO PUMLUMON FAWR - The Mountain Route

The Nant y Llyn is followed on its eastern bank to its source, Llyn Llygad Rheidol, an impressively-situated tarn crowded by the mountain's forbidding Ordovician cliffs. After circling the east and south shores of the tarn, high grassy corridors lead up to the pass between Pumlumon Fawr and Fach from where a simple south-south-easterly ascent leads to the stony summit adorned with two large cairns, a trig point and a couple of shelters.

Being the highest mountain in the Elenydd region of Wales, Pumlumon Fawr has extensive and interesting vistas in all directions. The graceful arc of Cardigan Bay can be traced from the Lleyn Peninsula to the northern Pembrokeshire coast. Cadair Idris stands out boldly in front of the pale profiles of the distant Snowdonian giants in the north whilst, in the south, the great sandstone escarpments of the Brecon Beacons and Carmarthen Fan can be clearly distinguished in good conditions. At Pumlumon western foot the Nant-y-moch Reservoir and dam can be seen in their entirety amidst a mix of bare hills and spruce woods. The scheme was completed in 1963 and is part of the Central Electricity Generating Board's Cwm Rheidol Hydro-electric Scheme.

I have included three descents from Pumlumon's summit. The first is longer but takes in a couple of extra peaks whilst the shorter routes allow a wider choice of accommodation.

Descent via Pen Pumlumon Arwystli

By descending eastwards guided by a ridge fence, Pumlumon's finest view, across Llyn Llygad Rheidol towards Hyddgen and Cadair Idris, can be seen. From this angle the cwm's magnificent architecture can be best appreciated. I can remember arriving here at first light on a February morning and being transfixed by the translucent, pinkish light that penetrated the early haze, accentuating the russet mountain grasses. The light lent an air of mystery to the view in which the unlit north-facing crags still retained a sprinkling of snow from previous falls. It would be worth camping high on the mountain to see such a spectacle.

The path climbs a subsidiary grassy dome before rounding the crag studded Cwm Gwarin. It finally arrives at the huge cairns which crown the summit of Pen Pumlumon Arwystli. Looking northwards the terrain changes from green to brown, from grass to peat hag. More ancient cairns crown Carnfachbugeilyn and Pumlumon Cwmbiga leading the eye to the rugged Aran crests.

On the summit of Pumlumon Fawr

The route continues along the ridge for a short while. The spruce woods of the Hafren Forest come right to the top hereabouts. At GR 819884 the ridge is abandoned for a waymarked path eastwards down the grassy spur of Carreg Wen and into the forest. On reaching a T-junction of forestry roads turn right then follow the flinted roads on a zig-zag course round the deep cutting of the Afon Hore to exit at GR 828868. The flinted track continues southwards past an old mine to follow the narrow Wye Valley to the A44 at Pont Rhydgaled farm ¹/₂ mile west of the Glansevern Arms.

Alternative Descent via Eisteddfa Gurig

From the summit of Pumlumon the route normally described in guidebooks descends to the old mines to the south-east and is very dull indeed. A far better alternative is to follow Pumlumon's southern ridge where the walking on a gentle grassy incline is easy and includes airy views. At GR 786841 by the eastern edge of the Dyll Faen conifer woods a bridleway that has been turned into one of those unsightly bulldozed farm roads is encountered (the Pumlumon range has more than its fair share of these EEC sponsored roads). This descends to the roadside farm at Eisteddfa Gurig, where the main route is joined. The farm used to be a cafe which offered bed and breakfast and a campsite but unfortunately they do so no longer. The view now is one of rolling grassy hills, studded with the occasional crag and partially cloaked with dark spruce. These are lower hills - smoother and softer. They recline round the valleys of Wye and Tarennig while rivers and streams meander and weave amid pallid moorland tussocks.

Unless it's late or you're tired, in which case you may choose to use the road all the way to Pant Mawr, head for the gate at GR 800841: it is obscured until the last moment by a roadside crag. A short climb over rough tussocks brings you to a good, grassy miners' track that rakes across the southern slopes of Cribiau Eisteddfa-fach then descends to marshy ground to ford the Cyff (one low fence obstructs the footpath here). Just beyond the river crossing a stony track is met and followed into the Wye Valley below Y Drum. The shallow Wye needs to be forded (not easy in winter) before the route continues on another track which descends by its banks to the A44 road at Pont Rhydgaled. The Glansevern Arms is $^1/_3$ mile east and the Plynlimon Guest House a short way further.

Alternative Descent to Dyffryn Castell

The Dyffryn Castell Hotel to the west (GR 774817) offers fine alternative accommodation although it would involve a little road walking, or a route variation on the following day, to return to the described itinerary.

From the side of the Dyll Faen forest, instead of descending eastwards, as on the Eisteddfa Gurig route, continue south-westwards on a path which leads directly to the hotel on steep grassy slopes. The village of Ponterwyd (more accommodation) is just 2 miles further west on the banks of the Rheidol.

HENGWM TO PANT MAWR VIA NANT-Y-MOCH - A Foul Weather Route

This low route follows the track above the eastern shores of Nant-y-moch to Maesnant farm where it becomes a tarmac road. At GR 758848, a track to the left climbs along the steep grassy flanks of

Bryn-llwyd to the forest on Dyll Faen. Forest tracks then lead to the bridleway at GR 786841 on Pumlumon Fawr's southern ridge. Our route follows the old bridleway used on the previously described alternative descent to Eisteddfa Gurig.

FACT FILE

Distances and Time

Mountain route via Hafren Forest	19mls	30km	10 hours
Mountain route via Eisteddfa Gurig	17mls	27km	9 hours
			(to Pant Mawr)
Foul weather route	18mls	29km	9 hours
			(to Pant Mawr)
	16mls	25km	8 hours
			(to Ponterwyd)

Terrain
Largely moorland with some forest roads and, in the low-level route, tarmac

Accommodation (limited so book early - do not descend here without accommodation arrangements in place)
Inn and a B&B at Pant Mawr
Hotels & B&Bs at Ponterwyd
Inn at Dyffryn Castell
B&B at Cwmergyr, S of Eisteddfa Gurig (GR 795826)
Good wild camps - nearest official sites in Wye Valley at GR 890803.

Tourist Information
Aberystwyth. Tel 01970 612125/61195

CHAPTER 7

The Great Reservoirs
The Wye Valley to Elan Village

This section of the route begins with unexciting forestry slopes but ends with a splendid excursion above the impressive reservoirs and dams of the Elan Valley. Marred by the scars of mass afforestation the hillside south of the Wye Valley promises little, but the mood changes on the gritstone outcrops of Craig y Lluest, where views of the glaciated Ystwyth Valley to its west raise the spirits for the continuation down the desolate wastelands of High Elan.

Beyond Pont ar Elan, the expansive quiet waters of the Craig Goch Reservoir add a serenity to the landscape. It is, however, rudely interrupted at the dam where the overspill thunderously cascades as a white wall of water into the forested valley below. The power and presence of the Elan dams is an awe-inspiring sight which, though massively intrusive, curiously adds great character to the landscape.

South of Craig Goch, the contours converge and gritstone crags protrude above gorge-like valleys. Rock enthusiasts could not fail to be impressed by the cliffs of Graig Dolfaenog which rise precipitously from the wooded slopes above the Carreg-ddu Reservoir, nor by Craig y Foel, north of the Caban-coch Reservoir. The path that rises from Carreg-ddu to Y Glog Fawr gives memorable and contrasting views of both the Wye and Lower Elan Valleys before descending easily through a green and gentle landscape to the terminus at Elan Village.

PANT MAWR TO ELAN VILLAGE - The Main Route

To reach the Elan Valley the high, forestry-clad fells to the south of the Wye Valley must be scaled. The path starts inconspicuously about 400yds east of the Glansevern Inn on the A44. It is not signposted, but is easily pinpointed by its position opposite a wooden footbridge (GR 854821) spanning the River Wye, which meanders through flat green fields at the edge of the half-felled

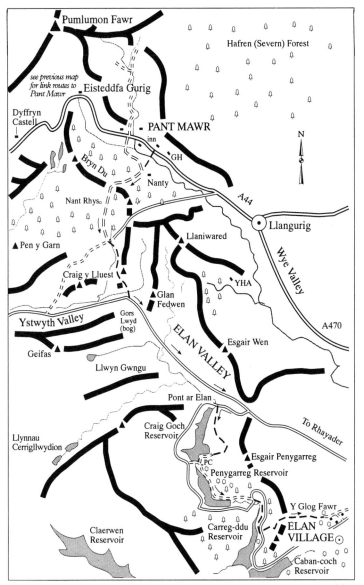

see previous map for link routes to Pant Mawr

Pumlumon Fawr

Hafren (Severn) Forest

Eisteddfa Gurig

Dyffryn Castell

PANT MAWR

inn

GH

N

Bryn Du

Nanty

A44

Nant Rhys

Llangurig

Pen y Garn

Llaniwared

Wye Valley

Craig y Lluest

YHA

Glan Fedwen

Ystwyth Valley

Gors Lwyd (bog)

ELAN VALLEY

A470

Geifas

Esgair Wen

Llwyn Gwngu

Pont ar Elan

To Rhayader

Llynnau Cerigllwydion

Craig Goch Reservoir

Esgair Penygarreg

PC

Penygarreg Reservoir

Y Glog Fawr

Claerwen Reservoir

Carreg-ddu Reservoir

ELAN VILLAGE

Caban-coch Reservoir

plantations of the Tarennig Forest. The path utilises the rickety old footbridge before heading southwards across the fields to the stone-built farmhouse of Nanty, surrounded by stands of spruce and larch.

A left turn along a track by the farm leads to a Forestry Commission road which climbs the northern side of the valley westwards and then south-west to gain the ridge at Bryn Du (GR 843807), where it briefly enters open fellside, giving views of Pumlumon on the northern horizon. The bridleway that follows the crest of the ridge is not navigable due to the Forestry Commission's overplanting within their boundaries and failure to provide stiles over the barbed wire perimeter fences. Shortly after re-entering the forest the path descends to cross the Afon Diliw close to the ruins of Nant Rhys. It then follows the widening and increasingly lively river which it fords just past the plantation's edge.

A southbound path passes east of the old farm buildings of Lluest-dolgwiail before rising up the steep grassy slopes towards Craig y Lluest. The path is little used and indistinct. Once the ridge is attained it is preferable to head southwards to the rock outcrops (GR 849759) in order to see striking views down the Ystwyth Valley towards the lead mines of Cwmystwyth. Two fine, craggy hanging valleys, Craig Cwmtinwen and Graig Ddu, interrupt the sweeping lines of the grass and bracken-clad hills that surround the river, which has cut a deep, craggy bed through their thin topsoils. A narrow tarmac ribbon, the Cwmystwyth to Rhayader mountain road twists along the southern side of the valley before fading from view beyond the mine ruins. An equally impressive view is seen northwards along the Diliw Valley where Pumlumon forms the skyline.

From Craig y Lluest a steep descent is made to the point where the mountain road bends south-east towards the Elan Valley. A wooden bridge is used to cross the now shallow Ystwyth. A great marsh, Gors Lwyd, lies between the two rivers. Here the Ystwyth is slowly stealing the waters of the Elan in an excellent example of river capture, a process which will take millions of years to evolve.

The mountain road is used for a quick and easy passage through the barren and scruffy landscapes of the wide upper Elan Valley. It is possible to follow the high hills to the east; they are common land

Craig Goch Reservoir and dam

with agreed access. Unfortunately the ground is tussocky and you would be walking against the grain of the land for much of the time.

The winding lane passes Bodtalog, once the scene of a turnpike fracas of the Rebecca Riots. On the night of October 9th, 1843 an old lady who collected tolls there was set upon by the rioters, one of whom fired a powder gun directly at her face injuring both eyes. Although able to identify her attackers she refused to do so in spite of the offer of a £50 reward for information. The fear of reprisal was too great - such was the vehemence of the Rebeccas. This area was recently the site of a proposed enlargement of the Craig Goch Reservoir, a scheme which was shelved (permanently I hope!).

The mountain road is left where it converges with the reservoir road which twists and rapidly descends to Pont ar Elan at the head of the Craig Goch Reservoir. From here a course along the eastern shores of the lake across wettish rough grassland, keeping to the left of the Water Board fence, leads to a wide, grassy cart track which rises high above the lakeshore. Craig Goch is more secluded than its neighbours and encircled by barren, grassy hills. However its lack of physical character is outweighed by its tranquillity and its indefinable, ethereal qualities.

After passing a ruined cottage the track becomes less well defined until it is joined by a green road from the ridge, Esgair Perfedd. It then descends to the massive Craig Goch Dam where the head of water cascades thunderously under thirteen arches to the river below. The hills, now craggy in places, close in on the L-shaped Penygarreg Reservoir. The moorland is now partially wooded, coniferous to the south and broad-leaved to the north. A stony track follows the eastern and then northern shores of the lake before reaching the next dam. From here, in the view to the east, expansive scree and cliffs tower to the skyline in a very impressive scene. This is Graig Dolfaenog.

At the northern extremity of the Carreg-ddu Reservoir a grassy track descends through an avenue of larch and spruce to the metalled reservoir road, which it crosses in order to reach the lakeshore path that used to form a bed for the track of the constructors' railway (the imprints left by the wooden sleepers are still evident in places today). Although this track is beautiful and leads to the Carreg-ddu Dam and causeway just 2 miles by road from Elan Village, the superior route leaves it at GR 914657. Here a stream can be seen tumbling down on a rocky course south of Graig Dolfaenog before feeding the lake. The narrow path rises up the heather slopes before crossing the stream and reaching the grassy ridge south of Y Glog Fawr. On the south-western horizon the pale moorlands rise to a curious flat-topped hill with prominent twin cairns. This 2,000-footer is Drygarn Fawr, one of the highlights of tomorrow's itinerary.

The path veers north-eastwards and descends on a wide track well-used by motorcycles. In the view ahead the beautiful valleys of the Elan and the Wye are visible in a landscape that is softer and more fertile than any seen since Machynlleth. A brook is crossed and the way is lined with hawthorn, oak, silver birch and bracken. It then enters a small copse before passing by the ruined farmhouse to reach a lane. A cart track leaves the lane at GR 939665 and descends to the B4518 a couple of hundred yards east of the Elan Valley Hotel and about 2 miles from the charming small market town of Rhayader, whose fine inns can offer good food and wine.

THE ELAN VALLEY RESERVOIRS

The Birmingham Corporation Water Act of 1892 permitted the construction of reservoirs in the Elan and Claerwen Valleys, which would satisfy the ever-growing demands for water by the city's industries.

In the first part of the scheme four reservoirs, namely Craig Goch, Penygarreg, Carreg-ddu and Caban-coch were constructed in the Elan Valley, producing a combined capacity of 11,000 million gallons. Filter beds were built east of the Caban Reservoir in order to extract the peat that would in time have blocked the 73 mile pipeline to the Franklin Storage Reservoir near Birmingham. The water flows the whole distance on this inclined pipeline under the forces of gravity.

A novel feature of the scheme helps preserve water supplies in times of drought. Between the reservoirs of Carreg-ddu and Caban-coch is a dam submerged 40ft below the high water level (above it a bridge conveys the motor road to Claerwen). Adjacent on the upstream side of the dam is the Foel Tower where water is drawn and conveyed by tunnel to the filter beds. The submerged dam helps maintain a level sufficient to keep the Foel Tunnel charged with water, whilst the lower Caban-coch lake would be used to discharge into the Afon Elan the mandatory 29,000 gallons a day required to keep the ecological status quo. The Dolymynach tunnel, whose inlet is near to an unfinished dam at the western end of Caban-coch, also supplements the Carreg-ddu levels by diverting to that reservoir (in times of drought) supplies from the Claerwen which would normally flow to Caban-coch.

Work commenced on the scheme in 1893 when a railway to supply men and materials to the sites of the dams was built, followed by the construction of a village to accommodate the multitude of workmen required for the project. The village included a school, hospital, mission hall and a licensed club.

The houses of Nantgwyllt and Cwm Elan, both of which have associations with the poet Shelley, were among the dwellings submerged by the reservoirs. It is said that Nantgwyllt was the subject of Francis Brett Young's novel *The House Under the Water*, and its garden walls can still be seen when Caban-coch's water levels are low. A church, chapel, school and numerous farms were

Historical print of the engine and drivers used for the construction of the Elan Reservoirs

Historical print of the construction of the Caban Coch dam, Elan Valley

submerged when the scheme was completed in 1904. It was inaugurated by King Edward VII.

The Claerwen Scheme was postponed until after the Second World War. In the original scheme it had been decided to build three reservoirs (the unfinished Dolymynach Dam was to have contained the lowest) but the new scheme made provision for only one - the Claerwen with a huge capacity of over 10,000 million gallons. It was completed in 1952 and inaugurated by Queen Elizabeth II and the Duke of Edinburgh.

FACT FILE

Distances and Time
Pant Mawr to Elan Village   17mls   28km   8 hours

Terrain
Some forest roads and tarmac lanes, then moorland trek and good lakeside paths

Accommodation (limited so book early)
B&B at Pengarreg shores
Hotel at Elan Village
Hotels, campsites and B&Bs at Rhayader (3 miles off route)

Tourist Information
Llandrindod Wells Tel 01597 822600

CHAPTER 8

Abergwesyn Common and the Tywi Valley

Elan Village to Rhandirmwyn

Unrivalled for aesthetic appeal, this section is characterised by its superb wild valleys and rushing streams, and the sheer variety of its scenery. Elan's charms are manifested for the last time in fine elevated views from the slopes of Gro Hill. The low route follows the Rhiwnant and Nant Paradwys Valleys to Bwlch y Ddau Faen, a high pass on the Abergwesyn Common that descends the lonely moors to Abergwesyn village.

The high route diverts down the upper Rhiwnant Valley to its zenith on Drygarn Fawr, a high eminence whose craggy top is endowed with two huge beehive cairns, visible for many a mile. It then descends either by the Gwesyn or Irfon Valleys to join the low route at Abergwesyn.

From here the way ahead is on empty moorland to Llyn Brianne, a much newer reservoir than its Elan neighbours. With steep conifer-clad slopes surrounding its sinuous shorelines, Brianne lends to this corner of Wales a Norwegian fjord-like character. South of the 300ft dam the Tywi resumes its natural course, flowing boisterously through a group of little known hills whose splendour and alpine character far outweigh their modest proportions. The area is a haven for buzzards, redstarts, raven, pied flycatchers and a rare bird of prey, the red kite.

Two possible routes are offered through these hills. The shorter and less demanding encircles the rocky oak-covered peak of Dinas and follows the turbulent Afon Tywi, passing close to its impressive confluence with the Doethie, whose lower reaches are explored more intimately by a second route. This route has previously crossed the dam and traced Brianne's south-western shore before descending to Troed-rhiw ruddwen. The Tywi is pacified as its valley widens and it is almost subdued when meandering amongst

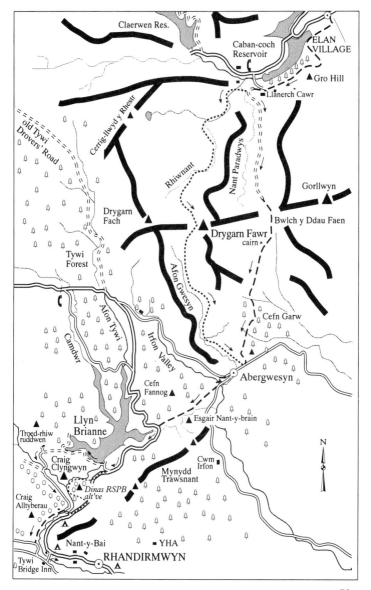

the sleepy pastures of Rhandirmwyn and its outlying hamlet, Nant-y-Bai. Here in ideal riverside settings are three campsites served by two delightful country pubs, the Tywi Bridge Inn and the Royal Oak.

ELAN VILLAGE TO RHIWNANT - The Main Route

At Elan Village the river flows over a stony bed beneath the oakwoods and crags of Cnwch. Towering above the river, the Caban-coch Dam is an alien giant, especially impressive when the reservoir's headwaters spill over its stone ramparts.

The route crosses the Elan at GR 931648 on a white suspension bridge and continues along a track leading south-westward through the woods. After about 50yds the track is left for one that zig-zags up the slopes to reach a metalled lane terminating at the dam's edge. The path now follows the bouldered shoreline of the reservoir before climbing the slopes of Cnwch alongside the forest of larches that cloaks Gro Hill. These two hills are divided by the Nant y Gro which flows from the wet grassy slopes of Y Gamriw. Retrospective views from Cnwch's slopes include a magnificent vista across the Caban-coch Reservoir, with its dam and causeway dividing it from the Carreg-ddu lake.

Beyond the forest the edges of a really wild area are entered. The lower slopes of Y Gamriw are boulder-strewn and bracken-covered, decorated with isolated, dwarfed trees. A single stand of pine borders an old ruined cottage (GR 927632) which is passed before the path veers south-west. After fording the Nant y Gro, the route rejoins the forest's edge to the north of Gro Hill where a wide, short-grassed track descends luxuriously and delightfully to Llanerch Cawr farm which is situated at the south-western extremity of the Elan Valley reservoirs.

Beyond Llanerch the route enters the valley of the Claerwen. After following a metalled road on the river's southern banks for about 50yds, a farm track leads from a gate on the left-hand side to the Rhiwnant's lovely twisting valley, memorable for its wild solitude and serenity. The scene is at its most magnificent outside the summer months when, on a sunny day, the withered brackens are transformed into a flame red mantle to the hills that flank the

Llyn Llygad Rheidol and the northern slopes of Pumlumon Fawr
(high route - Chapter 6)

On the low route north of Abergwesyn (low route - Chapter 8)

bustling river. A small stand of pine trees complements the ruggedness of the surrounding landscape - a far cry from the endless conifer regiments of nearby plantations.

There's a choice of routes to Abergwesyn. If the weather is settled it's better to head for Drygarn Fawr and the highest ground: if not there's a foul-weather route via Nant Paradwys and Bwlch y Ddau Faen.

RHIWNANT TO RHANDIRMWYN VIA DRYGARN FAWR - The Mountain Route

The farm road is left where it veers southward alongside the Nant Paradwys. After fording this stream near its confluence with the Rhiwnant our less obvious route continues up the south side of the Rhiwnant Valley. The increasingly lively river's left banks are followed past some derelict mine workings. The winding valley narrows as it rises through the now more craggy and rough slopes of Drygarn Fawr where the path degenerates into a sheep track.

The Rhiwnant's banks are left at GR 873598, where a stream flowing from the ridge between Drygarn Fawr and Carreg yr Ast is followed to its source near the crags that mark the position of the latter peak. From here turn right taking a south-westerly course for Drygarn's two huge beehive cairns which crown the highest summit between Pumlumon and the Brecon Beacon/Carmarthen Fan escarpment to the south. These massifs are easily recognisable on a mist-free day in an expansive and interesting, if unspectacular, panorama enlivened by views of the upper recesses of the Elan Valley reservoirs.

A south-westerly route from Drygarn Fawr will lead to the upper valley of the Afon Gwesyn, whose course is followed until it meets the Irfon at Abergwesyn. This route is arduous in its upper reaches, the sometimes wettish ground being covered in thick tussocky grass but, as the valley deepens, a well-trodden path develops, leading the walker into a beautiful twisting gorge, 2 miles in length. Many broad-leafed trees decorate the bracken-clad stony slopes whilst the river itself is lined with wind-bent hawthorn. The newly built farm track encountered leads to Trysgol. From here the path descends the ensuing steep, wooded valley and on leaving the woods crosses a field, joining a rutted cart track near to the Gwesyn, which it fords a little further down river.

The track meets a tarmac farm road and a left turn here will lead to the Beulah-Abergwesyn road by the tiny post office/general store. The route continues along the westbound road which crosses the River Irfon at Abergwesyn. The main valley is left by a forestry road at the far side of the bridge. It winds steeply up the hillside before entering the southern edge of the vast Tywi plantations, which blanket some 30 square miles of hills stretching northwards to Strata Florida. The forestry road is quit just prior to its entry into the plantations and the new path, from its left-hand side, leads down to a large house which was once the Llwyn-derw Hotel. From here it continues along the featureless, grassy valley of the Nant-y-brain. This area has recently been the subject of great controversy. The Forestry Commission wanted to extend their Tywi plantations but were eventually defeated after a strong campaign by the Ramblers' Association.

After the crossing of Nant Rhyd-goch climb on the path which zig-zags up Cefn Fannog. The map has it going westwards into the forest but you can follow the grassy spur parallel to the Nant-y-brain until that stream veers southwards around the skirts of Pen y Foel. The route maintains its south-westerly direction to the top of the pass north of Esgair Garn before descending to a road which contours around one of the scruffier fingers of the Llyn Brianne Reservoir.

Llyn Brianne, completed in 1972, holds 13,400,000 gallons of water to ensure an adequate supply to the Swansea area. Its expanse is more obvious from further along the road to the south-west, from where the spruce-lined flooded valleys of the Camdwr and Tywi seem to recede like serpents to the barren Elenydd skyline.

At Bwlch-y-fin (GR 794482, not marked on the 1:50,000 map), which is at the head of a verdant, fertile vale, a road to the right is taken and the lake's massive stone-fill dam and outfall are seen. (At the time of writing Bwlch-y-fin farm does B&B.) To the left the Tywi resumes its course in a fine, rugged V-shaped valley.

The main route continues over the dam and then follows a forestry road around the lake to its western extremity. Here another forestry road heads south-west, descending to Troed-rhiw ruddwen in the beautiful Doethie Valley. As the farm is passed, the stark cliffs of Craig Pysgotwr appear above the lush pastures that surround the tree-lined Doethie river. The path joins a narrow tarmac lane as the river turns 90 degrees beneath Craig Clyngwyn, revealing a scene of bracken and a myriad oaks clothing the hillsides: a wonderful autumn sight. We are now in the midst of RSPB areas and a look to the skies could well reveal the rare red kite, regularly seen in this vicinity.

The lane follows the western banks of the Doethie until, in one of this walk's finest scenes, the powerful foaming torrents of the Tywi force their way through a narrow bouldered gorge between the Dinas and Craig Clyngwyn (on 1:50,000). A rock outcrop hereabouts gives a fine platform from which to view this cataract and its confluence with the lively, if more subdued, Afon Doethie. Half a mile further, the lane crosses the Tywi to meet the road from Llyn Brianne but it is forsaken for a track which follows the west side of the valley passing Gallt-y-bere farm and camping site. The Tywi is below and to the south, flowing on a wide bed through green pastures. As the river turns southwards a very narrow country lane is encountered which descends steeply, crosses a tributary of the Tywi and ascends just as steeply to meet another lane. A left turn here will lead to the Tywi Bridge Inn, a whitewashed building near the riverbank and opposite a steel bridge. A backdrop of spruce and larch on the hillside which rises from the back garden, and the smattering of colour provided by the owner's peacocks, complete a charming rural scene.

There is a campsite at Bron-y-cwrt farm (across the bridge in the fields to the right) but for those requiring more luxury there is the Royal Oak at Rhandirmwyn, $1^1/2$ miles down river.

Rhiwnant to Abergwesyn via Bwlch y Ddau Faen and Carnau - Foul Weather Alternative

Continue along the stony track from the Rhiwnant Valley which veers left to climb Nant Paradwys, a pleasant upland valley which shallows, and transforms to wilderness as height is gained.

At the termination of the track continue across rough open moorland to Bwlch y Ddau Faen, a wild moorland col. Do not worry too much if you lose sight of the intermittent paths (sheep tracks) through the peat; take compass bearings and make sure that you

*The ancient cairn on Carnau, Abergwesyn Common with
Drygarn Fawr on the horizon*

round the eastern side of Cedni's wide hollow. A couple of concrete
posts should act as a guide to the large cairn and wind-shelter on the
hill named Carnau - a good place for a refreshment stop.

From the cairn a faint track heads south-westwards with the
view ahead dominated by rocks of Creigiau Duon and the large
spruce forest of Cefn Garw. It's important to locate the easy fording
place over Nant Gewyn (GR 886574). Further south the rocky ravine
becomes deep and the river treacherous, with numerous waterfalls.
The place you want is roughly at the point where the stream
changes direction to flow from south-east to south. You may also
spot a sunken, reedy path while descending to the far banks at this
point.

The path descends further across the moors to the spruce forest,
where a small metal gate marks the entry. A good track descends
through the trees to ford a stream, Nant Melyn, where a flinted
forestry track takes over and climbs towards Cefn Garw. Watch out
for the grassy forest ride at GR 882556 (there are a couple of
'pretenders' preceding the bend). If you are unsure or miss it, turn

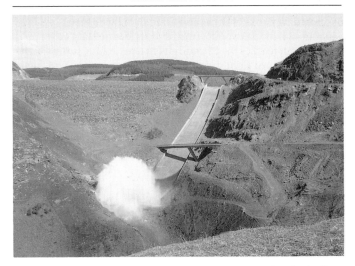

Llyn Brianne Dam

right at the next crossroads to reach the gate at the plantation's edge. A left turn is made through another gate and downhill across fields. A rutted track develops which, in turn, becomes a muddy tree-lined track passing close to a whitewashed farmhouse (but not as close as the map shows). It fords a stream flowing from a crag-fringed gorge in some delightful woodland above the farm and climbs out to high pastures, which are traversed with a fence to the left. Go through a gate in the fence (GR 869543) and continue along a stony track descending through the sylvan hollow north of Bryn Clun. After passing through a farmyard the lane meets the Abergwesyn road just to the east of its old post office where the high route is joined.

Llyn Brianne to Rhandirmwyn, an alternative via Dinas

This takes the Brianne-Rhandirmwyn lane in favour of the more intricate main route. It includes a circuit through the nature reserve and provides a beautiful alternative way which should not be lightly dismissed, especially if limbs are tiring or time is short. The path around Dinas starts by the chapel at Ystradffin, passes over wetlands to reach the banks of the Afon Tywi as it squeezes between the crowding flanks of Dinas and Craig Clyngwyn, then threads its way through the oakwoods, around rocks, past nesting boxes until it once again reaches the Rhandirmwyn lane. A little further along the lane you turn right dipping to a bridge over the Tywi. Here, beneath the steep, partially wooded slopes of Craig Alltyberau, the main route is rejoined.

FACT FILE

Distances and Time

Low route	23mls	34km	11 hours
Mountain route via Gwesyn Valley	26mls	42km	13 hours

Terrain
High featureless moorland traverses on all routes plus forest roads, field paths and lanes

Accommodation
B&B at Bwlch-y-fin (Llyn Brianne) - reduces section by 6 miles (10km)
B&B campsites and bunkhouse at Nant-y-Bai
Inn, B&B and campsite at Rhandirmwyn

Tourist Information
Llandrindod Wells Tel 01597 822600

CHAPTER 9
The Tywi Valley and the Foothills of the Black Mountain
Rhandirmwyn to Llanddeusant

Laid before us is another day of beautiful countryside on footpaths and country lanes through verdant meadows and shapely hills to Llanddeusant, a small village at the foot of Mynydd Du (the Black Mountain).

Rather than follow lanes from Rhandirmwyn to Llandovery, two rather devious hill routes are offered which are preferable in that they open up views invisible from the valley floor. One begins from Nant-y-Bai and ascends the slopes of Mynydd Mallaen. A second route follows the Tywi's banks for a mile before climbing to the eastern side of the green hills of the Fforest Ridge before descending a quiet country lane to Llandovery.

More country lanes are used in the approach to Myddfai before a low moorland traverse to Llanddeusant, where there is an inn, youth hostel and campsite.

RHANDIRMWYN TO LLANDDEUSANT - The Main Route

From Rhandirmwyn it will be tempting to follow the attractive leafy lanes that lead to Llandovery. However a far finer route traverses the eastern slope of Mynydd Mallaen where the views reveal so much more of the beautiful scenery than those from the valley itself where the lanes are densely hedged.

The forestry road that is used to climb the slopes of Mynydd Mallaen is 400yds along the Dolaucothi road from the Tywi Bridge Inn. As it leaves the lower plantations, the restricted views are transformed to airy scenes of the Tywi Valley around Nant-y-Bai, where the distant white cottages seem to be huddled for shelter at the foot of Cnwch, a small rounded hill separated from the northern hillsides by the Nant-y-Bai stream. Beyond Cnwch, the grey spoil heaps of a disused lead-mine, now surrounded by vast young conifer plantations, are a reminder of what was once a flourishing

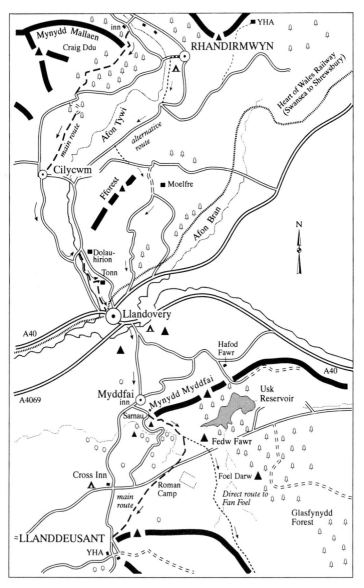

industry in these parts.

Near to the plantation's exit at Cwm-saethe an old track branches to the left of the forestry road. This in turn leads to a gate (GR 767442) at the edge of a high meadow across which the Brecon Beacons and Mynydd Du can be seen on the horizon. After maintaining a south-south-westerly direction over the meadow the Cwm Rhaeadr Plantations are entered and a narrow descending path is followed through the dark woods until it meets a wide forestry track at an acute angle. Glimpses of high waterfalls cascading from the Craig Ddu cliffs can be seen through gaps in the stands of spruce. The forestry road to be used leads south-westwards before switching back to a junction (GR 764427) where a right turn is taken. After turning left at the next junction and following the road southwards for a short while, a leafy path on its right-hand side descends to the Nant y Rhaeadr which it crosses via a wooden footbridge. The path then climbs to a cart track meeting a country lane at GR 762422 opposite a small terrace of cottages.

Three hundred yards southwards along the lane, a farm track on the left passes through a small forest. It ends at a farmhouse but a path to the west of it goes to the top of a hill, Penfedw Fawr, which stands alone between the merging valleys of Tywi and Gwenlais, providing an excellent vantage point. The northern and western prospects are dominated by Mynydd Mallaen whose expansive slopes are severed by the deep gorges cut by the Gwenlais and its tributary, the Merchon, whilst another of its streams tumbles down the rocky cwm by Craig Rhosan creating what is, after a period of rainfall, a magnificent waterfall. To the south is the village of Cilycwm, quiet in its pastures and surrounded on three sides by gentle, green hills; it's all so different from the wild Elenydd landscapes of the previous day.

The path descends by the eastern boundaries of a small conifer forest and across fields to the village. A building worth noting here is the fifteenth century church of St Michael, secluded from the main street with its guttering of cobbles by fine, dark, mature yew trees.

Although there is a footpath along the eastern banks of the Gwenlais it is quicker and better to travel southwards along the twisting country lanes back into the main valley of the Tywi. At Dolauhirion bridge, the Tywi is crossed. It is feasible to follow the riverside path into Llandovery via Tonn farm or the continue along the lanes.

Llandovery was described by that famous traveller of a century ago, George Borrow, as 'the pleasantest little town in which I have halted in the course of my wanderings'. It is known in Welsh as Llanymyddfri - 'the church amongst the waters' and was once occupied by the Romans whose fort, Alabum, was sited near to St Mary's church by the Afon Bran to the north of the town. The castle, built for the Norman baron Richard Fitz Pons in the twelfth century, was captured by the Welsh in the Glyndwr Revolts. In 1532 its owner Rhys-ap-Gruffydd was executed at the hands of Henry VIII for treason and, in an act of revenge by the Welsh, the castle was destroyed never to be rebuilt.

The town's history is intertwined with the fortunes of the cattle drovers who were so important in the rural communities before the railway age. When thieves made travelling on Wales' lonely and rugged roads a hazardous exercise, the local farmers hired them to drive cattle to the more lucrative markets of England and to settle for them accounts with non-local people. This meant that drovers needed to handle large sums of money and led to the introduction of banking systems - some of them even issuing bank notes. One of the most successful of these was David Jones' Black Ox Bank' which eventually had offices in Llandovery, Llandeilo and Tregaron before being taken over at the turn of the twentieth century by Lloyds Bank. Modern day Llandovery has two cafes and numerous public houses to replenish the needs of body and soul, and it may be with regret that it is left on the Brecon-bound A40.

You aim for Myddfai next. It is feasible to climb on the footpath up the little hill to the south of the town; indeed it has really good views. This route would continue through the conifer plantations of Llywynwormwood to GR 757311 a mile to the west of the village. The 3 miles of hedge-lined country lanes between Llandovery and Myddfai, however, are very pleasant. Few cars would be seen on this journey and those in a hurry to get to the mountains would be advised to follow this line. A right turn from the Brecon road along the lane signposted 'Myddfai' leads across the Afon Gwydderig at the Waterloo Bridge and, after maintaining direction at the crossroads (GR 776339), the winding lane climbs the rolling hilly country amongst sylvan landscapes.

Myddfai has a picturesque church with a fourteenth century

Llandovery Square

font and references to the legendary Physicians of Myddfai (see Lady of the Lake - next chapter). The Plough Inn next door has one of the most impressive bars I have seen. It has been converted from an old barn and has a gigantic stone fireplace. Its high roof-line is spanned by dark oak beams and roof trusses.

It is possible to use either of the two lanes from the village to Llanddeusant - they are both pretty. If you are in a hurry or want to camp at the official site owned by the Cross Inn (GR 773258) take the western one which weaves through verdant hill and vale past Talsarn and finally into Llanddeusant.

But the one that leads south-eastwards to the foot of Mynydd Myddfai is even more picturesque. It can be abandoned after a mile beyond Sarnau farm for a track which climbs the western outliers of the Mynydd Myddfai ridge and rounds the hillsides to Fedw Fawr. The wooded valley of the Clydach lies to the right and the highest peaks of Mynydd Du (the Black Mountain) cap the pallid moors ahead.

The track becomes less well defined and is little more than a green ribbon through the moors as the Clydach Valley shallows and bends to the south-west to meet the Trecastell (Trecastle) mountain road at GR 804266. Turn right along the road here past the earthwork remains of a Roman marching camp. Just short of the moorland boundary the route follows a track to the left which heads south then south-westwards above the Afon Llechach (stream). It soon joins the top edge of the field system then turns right along a track beyond a gate (GR 288256) to descend by a stream towards some woods. Turn left just before reaching them along a track which declines to the road just east of the cluster of buildings that form the centre of Llanddeusant.

The church of two saints, St Simon and St Jude, dates back to the early fourteenth century but was built on the site of a much earlier monastic community said to have been founded by the sons of the Irish king, Brychan Brycheiniog. There is also a youth hostel, formerly the Red Lion pub. It may provide a stopping place at the end of a short day from Rhandirmwyn but couldn't they have had it next door to the pub? (That is one mile north at GR 773258.)

Alternative route from Rhandirmwyn to Llandovery via Fforest Ridge

This route is more direct than the itinerary through Cilycwm and will suit those who are looking for a quicker way to Llandovery so as to leave more time for Mynydd Du. It begins by heading south along the banks of the Tywi from the Camping Club entrance (GR 778436) through a complex of fields and copses.

Shortly after fording a streamlet on stepping stones the path veers from the riverbank following the direction of a stand of trees and then a wire fence. Beyond a small stile a bracken-lined track then climbs through scrubland to the foot of a wooded hill (not named on the 1:50,000 map but south of Penrhyn farm). A metal five-bar gate is used as an entry to a field whose left-hand corner is to be reached before turning right (south-east) on an obvious track through woodland to reach a country lane at GR 781422.

The lane is followed to Dinas Bach, a mile to the south, where a path crosses south-eastwards across a field. It reaches a very narrow lane, which $1/2$ mile to the east is left for a farm road marked 'Moelfre'. The tarmac lane becomes a gated dirt track and views of the wide green valley of the Afon Bran are lovely, as is the pleasant little wooded dell fronting Moelfre farm. The road heads south to a fork (GR 785395) where a delightful winding lane heads south-west down attractive hill slopes high above Llandovery, revealing panoramas of the meandering Afon Bran and the tree-clad heights further distant. As it descends, the hedges obscure the scenery beyond, although glimpses may be had through the occasional farm gates. The narrow lane meets the busy A483 ¹/₂ mile north-east of Llandovery.

Myddfai direct to Mynydd Du at Fan Foel

Those who do not want to delay their journey at Llanddeusant can head straight for the mountains by diverting from the Sarnau track at a hairpin bend (GR 803278). From here they should tackle Fedw Fawr, a grassy hill overlooking the Usk Reservoir and its surrounding forest, then head east-south-east for Pont'ar Wysg where forest meets road.

The largely trackless route southwards over undulating rough moor is highlighted by the odd cairn and the scant remains of stone circles. Gradually Fan Foel rises supreme above a moorland sea and

Craig-y-nos Castle, upper Swansea Valley

is tackled head on up its grassy nose: crags guard both its east and west faces. Fan Brycheiniog, the highest in the range, lies a short way to the south and, for those requiring shelter for the night, it is a rather splendid walk from there down the Fan Hir ridge into the Swansea Valley at Craig-y-nos. The old Snowdonia to Gower route followed this itinerary.

Next day this would necessitate either a low-level route over Cribarth to Cwmgiedd or Cwmtwrch-uchaf or a rough high-level crossing of Carreg Goch and Carreg Lem before meeting the high route at Tyle Garw.

FACT FILE

Distances and Time

Main route via Cilycwm	18mls	28km	9 hours
Alternative route via Fforest Ridge	15mls	24km	8 hours

Terrain
Country lanes, forest roads, field paths and a little easy moorland

Accommodation
Hotels, B&Bs and campsite at Llandovery
Inn at Myddfai
Campsite and youth hostel at Llanddeusant

Tourist Information
Brecon Tel 01874 3366

CHAPTER 10
Over the Black Mountains
Llanddeusant to the Aman Valley

Laid before us at the start of the day are the distinctive escarpments of Mynydd Du (The Black Mountain). The steep facades, carved from red sandstone, have been eagerly anticipated since their first sighting from Pumlumon.

The main route climbs on high moorland sheeptracks to Fan Foel where moorland becomes mountain. The smooth grassy slopes give way in the north and west to eroded tawny cliffs, layered with gritstone strata and broken by tight cwms. From the top a superb ridge walk along firm quartzite beds leads to Fan Brycheiniog, the highest peak in South-West Wales. A high mountain traverse follows, westwards along the cliff edges at first then over seldom trod fells to the Aman Valley.

When the clouds hang low on the hills this route is not easily navigated and it is best to use the bridleway southwards from Llanddeusant, climbing almost to the limestone peak of Carreg yr Ogof before dropping down into the Twrch Valley and through a little limestone gorge to Cwmtwrch-uchaf. Here there is a choice of routes, either to the Aman Valley or to the Lliw Hills.

LLANDDEUSANT TO THE AMAN VALLEY - The Main Route

Llanddeusant is a straggling village set in verdant rolling pastures parcelled by copse and hedgerow. Topping the rolling foothills are the cliffs of Bannau Sir Gaer (Carmarthenshire Beacons). On this route we aim for the western limestone peaks, starting with Carreg yr Ogof.

A pretty hedge-lined lane descends from the youth hostel past Cwmsawdde farm to cross the Afon Sawdde (river) where lovely woodland of oak and birch abounds. The lane now climbs steeply towards Gellygron farm. It is abandoned for a waymarked bridleway (left) just short of the farm. This track, which can be a little muddy initially, climbs uphill through an avenue of willow and birch decorated by holly, ivy, bramble, foxglove and wild primrose. It reaches a gate and step stile at the edge of the open moor. The impressive escarpments of Picws Du and Fan Foel command attention but our route aims southwards for the left edge of Carreg yr Ogof, a grassy shapeless mound from this vantage.

A patch of short-cropped grass obscures the initial path but just beyond it it appears as a green ribbon through rough grassy moorland speckled with crowberry. The path deteriorates into intermittently faint wheeltracks in the moor and climbs south to skirt the craggy eastern flanks of Carreg yr Ogof. Do not get too far away from the crags or your way over the col will be obscure and burdened by tussocks and peat hag. You may wish to detour to Carreg yr Ogof's trig point and splendid limestone crags that crown the summit. Views back are limited only by the atmospheric haze. I have seen Cadair Idris on a clear winter's day. On most days you should be able to see Pumlumon across the patchwork of field, forest and rolling hills.

If you climb the peak it will be necessary to retrace your steps to the bridleway which fords the Twrch Fechan (stream) at GR 785208. Just beyond the path divides. Take the less well defined course to the right. This heads southwards parallel with the stream. By now you really *are* in the middle of nowhere - this is big country; wild horses graze on the pallid windswept moors which yawn to little-known craggy peaks. To the right are the huge stony sides of Garreg Las and to the left the now less distinctive outlines of the Fannau (the main ridge). Ahead the hills huddle round the tight valley of the Twrch and channel our vision to glimpses of the Swansea Valley.

The map shows a junction of bridleways at GR 787193: the moors show no such thing. Be content to descend the crest of a moorland spur down to the Twrch Fechan. The ford shown does exist. Ribs of red sandstone make the crossing a doddle, which is more than can be said of the one across the Twrch proper. In summer it's OK, in winter you will get your feet wet.

From here you can either trace the top edge of Tyle Garw's limestone cliffs or go through the gorge itself along the eastern banks of the stream - the latter is a bit of a scramble in places. Either way you should aim for the footpath above some tree-lined spout-like waterfalls at GR 774154. Beyond the falls the path becomes a faint cart track almost lost in the long grasses of rough pastureland. It heads southwards to the ruin of Dorwen farm, where, sadly, the cracked walls must surely collapse.

A more prominent stony track takes over, descending to farmland and spruce forest to meet a metalled lane and a crossroads of tracks at GR 762125. A right turn down the lane leads to the Twrch, which is now a fast-flowing river. A footpath by an old mine railway heads southwards along its east banks to reach Cwm-twrch Uchaf, an austere industrial valley town situated in a deep glen at the confluence of the Afon Twrch and Nant Gwys. Cwm-twrch can offer two public houses and a few shops.

A path from the roadside at GR 757110 climbs south-west out of the Twrch Valley through pretty woodland offering impressive retrospective views of Garreg Lwyd and Foel Fraith, two of the Black Mountain peaks. A black-surfaced path leading from the exit of the woods to the lane which leads west to Rhiwfawr (Pen Rhiwfawr on pre-1985 maps) is a reminder that we are in coal-mining country.

Rhiwfawr, a weatherbeaten high hillside village, is passed and the route follows the steep gradient of the Rhydyfro lane until GR 742108 when a cart track on its northern side ascends the grassy ridge of Mynydd Uchaf. As the trig point is reached superb northern panoramas of the Black Mountain are revealed across the scars of the opencast coalfields and towns of the Aman Valley. In contrasting southern views the rounded townside hills of Pontardawe, Neath and Swansea form an interesting pattern, their moderate elevations being tamed by the expanding needs of urban and forestry development. On Mynydd Uchaf it is difficult to forget that we are in industrial Glamorgan, for its unkempt eastern slopes are littered with relics of our 'throw away' society - a rusty discarded fridge, the odd car tyre - signs that these hills are less cherished than their wild northern neighbours.

The cart track deteriorates and three closely grouped stone cairns are passed before a descent to a country lane at Cwm-nant Hopkin which leads down to the upper Clydach Valley. Beyond a line of electricity pylons it enters more cultivated pastoral countryside. There are views down to the now redundant anthracite coal-mine of Abernant tucked beneath the stark hills of Bryn Mawr

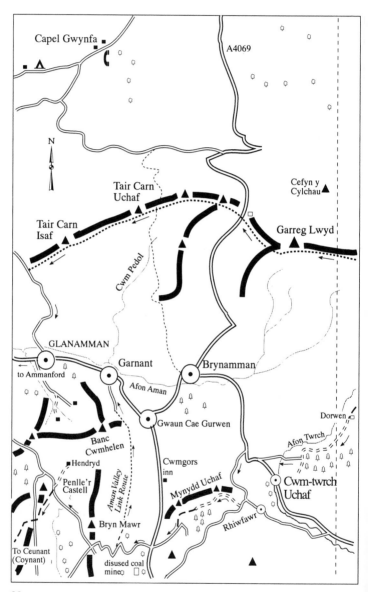

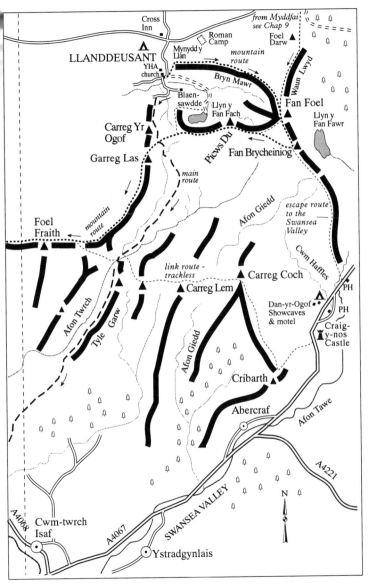

and Mynydd y Gwair which rise on the valley's western side. Trees that line the A474 help to obscure the colliery workings.

Accommodation needs will largely dictate where you go from here. Pontardawe and Swansea are a bus ride away but there is also Coynant farm (Ceunant on old maps) on the hills above - you could also ask permission to camp on the moors themselves.

Cwmgors to Coynant farm, Lliw Hills (Hills of Gower)

Those wishing to press on to the Gower or staying at Coynant farm (GR 647070) could follow the lane past the old colliery. It zig-zags up the hillsides of Bryn Mawr to a crossroads. Turn right and follow the road to the earthworks on Penlle'r Castell for a good view of the Aman Valley and Mynydd Du. If this is too circuitous you could turn left along the moorland track (black dashes) from Penlanau. Either way, aim for the path across the golden grassy hills to the well-defined track to the north of the Upper Lliw Reservoir, a rectangular lake surrounded with sleek hills faintly fringed with crag.

Follow the track to Mynydd Garn-fach and see the next chapter for the onward route. (Turn right down the prominent track at GR 654067 then right again into the cwm for Coynant.)

LLANDDEUSANT TO THE AMAN VALLEY - The Mountain Route

Retrace yesterday's main route for a short way down the little lane signposted to Llyn y Fan and on the grassy tree-lined track as far as a stile by the ford at GR 783248. Here a courtesy path marked by a white arrow at present heads westwards along the right-hand edge of a field to emerge on the open moorland west of Mynydd y Llan. A rutted path, formerly an old miners' corpse road, now continues along the southern lip of the moorland ridge. It's the best place of all to view the sculpted cliffs of Bannau Sir Gaer for they are seen to perfection above the Sawdde Valley, whose rich emerald fields are divided by trees and thick hedgerows with several picturesque whitewashed farmhouses peeping out from streamside copses. The spirit is rejuvenated at the prospect of some more high mountains, the first since Pumlumon.

The track stays just to the south of Bryn Mawr's top then climbs

Tair Carn Uchaf on the western ridge of Mynydd Du

south-eastwards, disappearing into the moor grasses of Waun Lwyd. By this time Fan Foel will be clear in your sights, rising from the moors like a beached whale. Passing close to the source of the Usk the route re-appears on the last grassy ramp to its summit. Now you get more intimate views along the line of cliffs which at their far end wrap around the secluded lake, Llyn y Fan Fach. The horizontal strata of the rust-coloured old red sandstone and grey millstone grit are typical of South Wales' Great Escarpment (collectively the Black Mountains, Brecon Beacons, Fforest Fawr and Mynydd Du) but the contrast between these landscapes and the more conventional mountain scenery of previous days in the north of the principality is unexpected.

It is possible to head south and westwards along the cliff edge but that way you would miss out Fan Brycheiniog, the highest mountain of the range. From the summit of Fan Foel to that of Fan Brycheiniog is $^{1}/_{2}$ mile of easy and pleasant ridge walking. The path keeps to the edge of the range's steep eastern ramparts and a second lake, Llyn y Fan Fawr, will be seen a few hundred feet below. The twin peaks of Pen y Fan and Corn Du in the Brecon Beacons should be easily spotted on the eastern horizon beyond the undulating ridges of Fforest fawr. The green-blue colours of the conifer-enshrouded Usk Reservoir refresh the pallid northern moors which fade to the patchwork of the Tywi Valley. There is also a handy stone wind-shelter on the summit - maybe a good time for a coffee break?

Next stop is Picws Du (the Black Peak, GR 812218 - not named on 1:50,000 maps). It can be done direct from Fan Brycheiniog (quicker) or by returning to Fan Foel and tracing the northern edge (more entertaining). Now you look down directly to Llyn y Fan Fach. It's an enchanting and dramatic place beneath the solemn shady cliffs and it has a tale to tell.....

THE LADY OF THE LAKE AND THE PHYSICIANS OF MYDDFAI

Rhiwallon, who was a son of the farmer of Blaensawdde farm, near Llanddeusant, was tending cattle near Llyn y Fan Fach when he saw a beautiful young maiden. He instantly fell in love with the girl, who was sitting by the lakeshore combing her long hair, and, offering her bread that his mother had prepared for his lunch, he asked her to marry him. She refused, saying that the bread was too hard and she vanished into the depths of the lake.

On the next day he brought a different type of bread but still it did not meet with her approval. On the third meeting his offering of unleavened bread was found acceptable and the girl agreed to marry him but attached one condition. She told him that she was not an ordinary mortal and that she would return to her kind if he struck her three times. Rhiwallon accepted her condition and they were happily married with three sons. The inevitable happened. It is said that the third time he struck her was after she had giggled at a funeral, and although it was hardly more than a tap, the lady of the lake disappeared from his life as mysteriously as she had first appeared.

The three sons however searched for her, and their efforts were rewarded when she appeared from the waters of Llyn y Fan Fach. She taught them about medicine and cures for the sick, showing them useful herbs from the mountainsides. The three boys became the first in a long line of Physicians of Myddfai. Many local doctors have claimed that they were related, the last being Dr C. Rice Williams of Aberystwyth, who died in 1842.

From Picws Du a descent should be made to Waun Lefrith. Here we leave the sandstone mountainscapes and head for the western tops which consist of limestone capped with gritstone. Descend westwards (no path) then climb to Carreg Yr Ogof where the limestone outcrops and crags are particularly impressive.

Intermittent paths descend to a grassy col before climbing southwards to the boulder-strewn, heather-splashed ridge of Garreg Las. The summit, known as Twyn-Swnd, is marked by two gigantic ancient tumuli and is a splendid place to view the vast expanses of the Black Mountain. Here you are right in the middle of the range - it's a remote wilderness with few signs of modern inhabitation and very few signs that walkers come here. The tops of the dark glaciated cliffs of Bannau Sir Gaer can just be seen to the north-west across pale rising moorland, and there are improving views southwards down the defile of Tyle Garw.

Descend by the western edge of the ridge, which is soon highlighted by immense slabs of gritstone. By contouring round the western scree slopes you'll come to Blaen Llynfell, an isolated pass sitting between Garreg Las and the rounded grassy Foel Fraith. It is easily recognised by its quarrying scars. Here amidst some boggy ground lie two small pools. To the north the graceful grassy flanks of Cefn y Cylchau fall to the deep hollow of Cwm Sawdde-Fechan, leading the eye to the beautiful rolling Carmarthenshire (Dyfed) hills beyond.

The path ascending Foel Fraith circumvents numerous shakeholes (surface hollows formed by collapsing underground chambers) on its way to the plateau-like summit. A descent of 300ft to Bylchau Rhosfaen precedes the short slog to the summit of Garreg Lwyd, which at 2,022ft is the highest top on this section of the walk. The summit is a distinctive place with huge stone shelters, and a stone-built trig point. The view northwards across the modest Carmarthenshire hills is now very expansive and it is possible, with care, to distinguish the peaks of Drygarn Fawr and Pumlumon on the horizon. Views to the south reveal the distant industrial valleys of the Aman and Upper Clydach squeezed between the barren Lliw Hills and Mynydd y Garth.

A north-westerly course across Garreg Lwyd's stony slopes leads down to the twisting A4067 at an altitude of 1,618ft. On this high pass are the disused Foel Fawr quarries and a car park.

The road is crossed and an ascent is made westwards on the southern slopes of Carn Pen-rhiw-ddu. Although it may seem logical from the map to aim for this summit and Carn Pen-y-clogau, this high line crosses ground that is rough and extremely marshy and it is better to take a parallel course across the southern slopes just above another marshy area on the lower slopes. The south-western section of the ridge is still rough in places, being thickly cloaked in heather with concealed boulders, but offers a much easier and drier passage.

After crossing a well-defined bridleway west of Carn Pen-y-clogau (GR 713183) it is best to aim directly for the large cairns of Tair Carn Uchaf which are said to date back to the Bronze Age. The craggy peak commands superb views to the coast beyond the Aman and Loughor Valleys. However, the most arresting aspect is that to the north, where Carreg-Cennen Castle is seen perched precariously on vertical limestone cliffs.

The castle, which was probably built in the twelfth century for Rhys-ap-Gruffydd, was captured by Owain Glyndwr in his struggles against the English. After the Wars of the Roses it was overrun by bandits who terrorised the neighbourhood until the Sheriff of Carmarthen drove them out.

The firm stony ridge is followed to Tair Carn Isaf before the steep south-westerly descent leads to a metalled lane (GR 675157) which can be utilised for further descent to Glanamman or Ammanford.

Wherever you stay in the Aman Valley there is the unique atmosphere of the industrial south which complements the previous rural charms. This is another piece in the Welsh cultural tapestry.

FACT FILE

Distances and Time

Main route to Coynant	20mls	33km	11 hours
Mountain route to Glanamman	16mls	26km	10 hours

Terrain
High moorland crossings on both routes. Paths intermittent

Accommodation
Inn at Cwmgors
B&B at Pen-y-Banc and Coynant
B&B at Garnswllt (2 miles S of Ammanford)
Inn at Ammanford

Tourist Information
Brecon Tel 01874 3366
Pont Abraham 01792 883838 (for Ammanford area)

CHAPTER 11

To the Coast
The Aman Valley to Swansea Bay

This section will be remembered for that first taste of the southern seashore, but its other attributes, if unspectacular, display the surprising diversity of the surrounding countryside.

On climbing out of the busy industrial Aman Valley a very different world is entered - that of the quiet expansive Lliw Hills (not named by the map-makers although christened the Hills of Gower by historian Wynford Vaughan Thomas). These high moors allow the first intimate views of the Gower Coast, thus strengthening further the resolve to press on aided by superb paths on smooth terrain.

Between Lliw and Gower is a relatively uninteresting expanse of semi-rural scenery where the route follows a complex network of paths through field and forest. However, there are some lovely peaceful corners. The Cwm-Llwyd oakwoods near Dunvant are a perfect example of nature thriving and deliciously decorating an area so close to less salubrious urban developments.

The lack of steep hills allows a very fast pace to be set through the suburbs west of Swansea, and the course of an old railway line provides an easy route through a wooded valley to Black Pill on the Swansea Bay.

THE AMAN VALLEY TO SWANSEA BAY - The Main Route

The bare hills of Lliw that tower above Glanamman are the last true range that bar the way to the Gower Coast. A lane (GR 670135) leading from the A474 starts the ascent through the picturesque cwm of the Nant Garenig. On its termination a farm track is followed south-eastwards to reach the open fellsides at Banc Cwm-helen, where the windswept grasses of Lliw seem to stretch as far as the eye can see. A south-westerly course then descends to the farm of Hendryd whose drive is used to reach a lane to the east of Penlle'r Castell, the earthwork remains of an ancient fort (not very

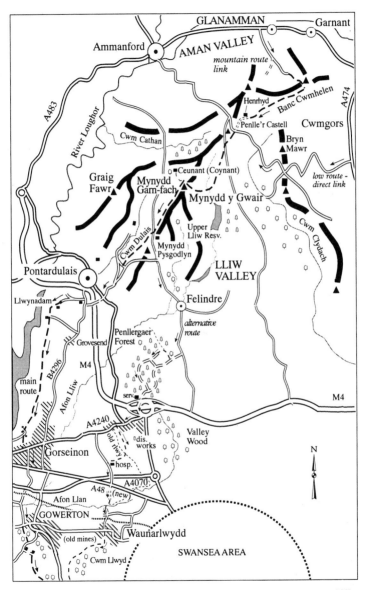

Passing the Upper Lliw Reservoir

impressive).

Opposite Hendryd's drive the path continues south-south-west across the golden grassy moors of Mynydd y Gwair giving views of the verdant Clydach Vale which contrasts so strikingly with the stark hills. A high unfenced lane is crossed (GR 667080) before descending slopes (no path marked) towards the Upper Lliw Reservoir. This small lake lies in a wild landscape only slightly tamed by the small spruce plantation on its eastern shores. A distinct rutted track to its north is followed to the west, descending briefly to cross the infant Lliw stream before rising boldly up the slopes of Mynydd Garn-fach.

From the cairned top and across the Lliw moorland the southern scenes are punctuated by cooling towers and scores of smoke-plumed chimneys in the industrial expanses that surround the Neath and Tawe rivers. Beyond them on the eastern side of Swansea Bay lies the giant complex of the Margam Steelworks whose future has for years been precariously balanced in the fickle hands of Whitehall administrators. Further west the marshes of the North Gower and the pastures west of Llanelli are divided by the Loughor estuary.

From Garn-fach's summit a south-westerly descent is made to reach a high unfenced lane (GR 638053) at the eastern end of Cwm Dulais, where a narrow tract of farmland at the valley floor bisects the wild moors. There are two possible routes from here to Dunvant, a suburb of Swansea.

Route 1: Via Cwm Dulais and Gowerton

By following the track high on the valleysides of Cwm Dulais this route misses out a stretch of tarmac. The road from the old coal mine is then encountered and this climbs over Bryn Bach Common and down to cross the busy A48 road. It then continues, offset slightly to the north, past a garden centre, under the M4 motorway to reach the Gorseinon road. Where you go now depends on the tide. During high tides turn left down the road then right down the lane to Grove End farm. This is the less interesting route, however, and if the tide is going to be out, it is best to turn right along the A road towards Pontardulais then left along the lane past Llwyndam farm and out onto the marshes of Morfa Mawr. The Llwchwr Estuary and its surrounding wetlands are straddled by the viaduct of the railway and the more modern motorway bridge. Vast pools may have been deposited by the outgoing tide. In the background the houses of Pontardulais are framed by the Lliw Hills you have just left.

The well waymarked route now heads southwards along the border of the marshes for a few yards, then across fields. It meets the terminus of a little lane at Grove End farm where the previously mentioned high tide route joins you.

The field paths are devious at times but the stiles are always there, as are the waymarking arrows. Two rather difficult ones have nearby gates. The path tries to dive for cover in a new housing estate but do not believe it; head southwards and you will find the next stile. By a second housing estate the route continues on a little hedge-lined track which emerges by Gwynfaen farm and stables. A left turn will lead past a house to a narrow metalled lane which should be followed southwards to a footpath signpost which points the way across more fields and then through a little ginnel to the A4240 road in the suburbs of Loughor.

Turn left along the road then right at the crossroads heading southwards through uninteresting housing, across the B road. The lane crosses the Afon Lliw, then goes under the railway and A484 in quick succession. You are on the edge of the coastal marshes again, although this time with the road as security. It passes a large caravan site before reaching the extremities of Gowerton.

A waymarked path begins straight across the road. It heads southwards through woodland by a little brook, which it crosses twice before settling for the western banks. The place becomes delightful. A wide variety of trees, shrubs and wildflowers co-exist in a mixture of woodland and wetland. A stile marks the exit into high fields and the path veers left to a pretty country lane that has

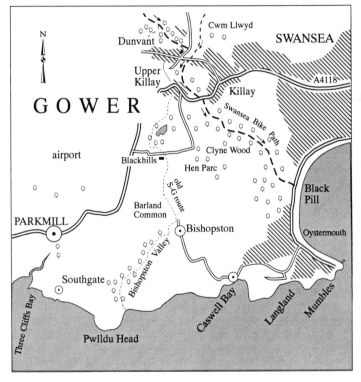

almost as many flowers as the woods. Turn right along the narrow, winding lane then left after ¹/₄ mile on a farm track signposted to Gellyeithrym. A footpath sign soon directs you to the right (south) over very marshy fields with scattered bracken and bramble. (Be prepared for a squelchy time during the winter months or use the path further on via Bevexe fach farm.)

The path gradually turns eastwards across drier fields at the edge of a narrow strip of woodland. Eventually it descends into a little valley to enter the woods. In a bracken-filled clearing (GR 588943) the main track veers right but this is not the right of way. Maintain your direction through more woodland by a streamlet. The path will lead you to the road at Dunvant adjacent to a social club. More importantly, there is a shop selling provisions and ice-creams next door, and a pleasant green with a seat on which to eat them.

Route finding from here to the coast couldn't be easier: a path from the bridge descends to the course of the old LMS Shrewsbury line. It has been tarmacked but it allows swift progress through 3 miles of pleasant woodland of the Clyne Valley to Black Pill. It has been designated as a cycleway but is used by many walkers.

Black Pill is a bustling place in the middle of the Swansea Bay. Views from its promenade encompass the sweeping coastline of Swansea, the more industrial scene of Port Talbot and beyond. The headland of The Mumbles with its lighthouse and pier lie in the opposite direction.

Route 2: Via Felindre and The Penllergaer Forest

The lane is followed south over the bare grassy hill of Pysgodlyn from where it descends to Felindre, a small, quiet village hidden in the depths of the now verdant Lliw Valley. A left turn is made by the church and the following lane climbs steeply to a junction (GR 638026) where the right fork taken leads southwards lined by pleasant tall hedgerow. The lane is, in turn, left at Fforest-newydd farm where a Forestry Commission access road is used to the edge of the Penllergaer Plantation. The next part of the route is not marked on the OS maps and was kindly shown to me by the chief forester, Bob Price.

After going through the boundary gate a left turn is made

following closely the track by the plantation's perimeter until GR 636013 (where the perimeter veers left) when the forestry track leads north-westwards amongst larch and spruce. At GR 632015 it meets the forestry road which is marked on the OS maps. This curves round steadily from its original westbound direction to assume a south-easterly one. It crosses a railway cutting and descends to Melinllan, a cottage by a small bridge spanning the Afon Llan, just a stream at this point. The forest is left on an approach road leading westwards to an M4 roundabout close to a new motorway services (accommodation if required). The large roundabout is crossed to the A48.

The original Snowdonia to Gower route continued through the glen of Valley Wood. Unfortunately this idyllic glen has fallen into the hands of developers and exits at the southern end have been barred. The A48 road is now followed from the motorway roundabout before continuing westwards on the A484 to Penllergaer - a total distance of about one mile. A left turn is made at Orchard Grove. A prominent path to the right then leads across grassland to a stony track heading southwards towards some derelict factory buildings. Just short of these a path heads south-south-west across a large area of Common Land, marked on the map as Mynydd Carn-Goch, to reach the grassy groove of the old railway. There are two distinctive paths hereabouts. One follows the course of the railway (south-east) but the one we need to use heads south-westwards towards the cottage-type hospital at the far end of the common. At another junction of paths the right fork is taken and this passes to the north of the buildings to reach Hospital Road at GR 608976.

We now turn right along the road and follow it over the newly constructed Llanelli Road to reach the old Swansea Road at GR 609971. After crossing this a farm track, staggered to the left, is followed southwards to its termination. A right turn (west) is now made, following the line of a hedge until a track leads down to the banks of the Afon Llan (river). The footbridge to be used lies a few yards to the right. A small marshy field is crossed to reach a tree-lined track, which heads south, crossing a metalled lane close to an aluminium works. It continues past several houses and turns right on reaching a green. A corner can be cut here, using a well defined path across the green. It rejoins the track (now a road) to the north

In the Tyle Garw Valley, Mynydd Du (low route - Chapter 10)
The cliffs of Bannau Sir Gaer seen from Picws Du (high route - Chapter 10)

of a railway bridge (GR 608956). Keep straight on across the main road through the housing estates of Waunarlwydd (pronounced Wine-AR-loyth) until you reach Caer-Gynydd Road where you turn right. Turn left into Westwinds Close and then at GR 604952 the urban sprawl is escaped for a period by a path (marked on OS maps with broken black line) which leads southwards across fields until it meets a well-defined east-west footpath beyond some hedgerow at the foot of the unnamed hill. This is followed westwards passing an ivy-covered stone chimney which is an air shaft for one of the numerous disused old coal mines in the area. Just after this landmark a narrow path on the left leaves the more obvious track and rises through thick bracken before turning south through mixed woodlands (GR 598947), a delightful sanctuary from the city that has spread on all sides. The woods are most beautiful during the early part of summer when many butterflies can be seen hovering on the varied species of wild flower that flourish beneath the twisted sessile oaks, lime and holly.

As the woods are left behind the track widens and straddles high meadows. Retrospective views to the north across the plains of Gorseinon include Valley Wood and Penllergaer Forest, and the pale hills of Lliw form the horizon.

A stony track now leads southwards to emerge at the B4296 between Dunvant and Killay (GR 596937) where a right (west) turn is made on the road which descends and passes over the course of a disused railway. This has recently been designated the Swansea Bike Path and offers the fastest passage to the coast. Winding for 2 miles through woodlands and pastures of the Clyne Valley it emerges on the coast at Black Pill on the wide sweep of Swansea Bay. It is good to breathe the sea air again. Tomorrow we visit Gower, known to many as 'the land of the setting sun'. It's a little bit of Cornwall come to Wales.

The Pennard Cliffs, Gower. (Chapter 12)

FACT FILE

Distances and Time

Main route via Gowerton (from Glanamman)	19mls	31km	9 hrs
Alternative route via Felindre (from Coynant)	14mls	22km	10 hrs

Terrain

A bit of everything; keep your compasses out for the field paths!

Accommodation

Wide range of accommodation in Swansea and The Mumbles

Tourist Information

Swansea Tel 01792 468321

Around the Gower: The Land of the Setting Sun
Swansea Bay to Three Cliffs Bay and the Extension to Rhosili

It is the last day. You have already completed a coast to coast: but this is the icing on the cake and it is a delicious mixture. Some will be content with the shorter promenade to Three Cliffs Bay with wonderful secluded inlets, tall limestone cliffs and a sand-blown castle; others, well they will want more of this fine peninsula and climb to Cefn Bryn, its backbone, and its highest top on Rhosili Down.

If time and the weather permit, then perhaps, when all is said and done, those golden sands of Rhosili *are* the most fitting place to end this long, long walk.

Three Cliffs Bay, Gower

BLACK PILL TO THREE CLIFFS BAY - The route

It seems a little strange after many days in the quietude of the hills to be walking along the populated seaside sands or promenade but it's good to be on the coast at last. This area is popular with surfers and wind-surfers alike. The beach here is a mixture of sand and mud so your exact route will depend on the tide and your own preferences.

The pier and lighthouse at The Mumbles will be clearly visible at the head of the bay but our route cuts inland at Oystermouth, climbing along the bustling shop-lined B-road signposted to Langland Bay.

Oystermouth Castle, which looms large to the right, has had a troubled

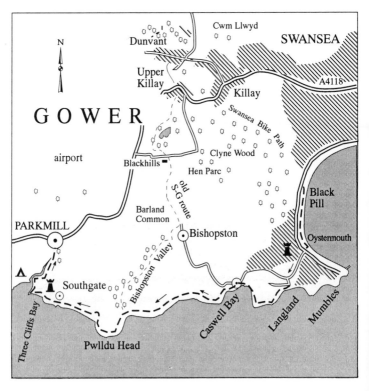

existence since its original construction by the Normans in about 1100. In fierce battles with the Welsh it has been destroyed more than once, the last time shortly after Edward I's triumphant two-day stay. The nearby Church of All Saints is reputed to have been built on the site of a Roman villa.

After dropping to the sandy inlet at Langland Bay we follow a pleasant path above the jutting coastal rocks but beneath the clifftops to Snaple Point then round Whiteshell Point into Caswell Bay. Caswell is a pretty little resort with cliffs ringing a small sandy bay, a few pines, a couple of hotels and an ice-cream stall. The scene gets wilder as you follow the path across bracken-clad slopes into

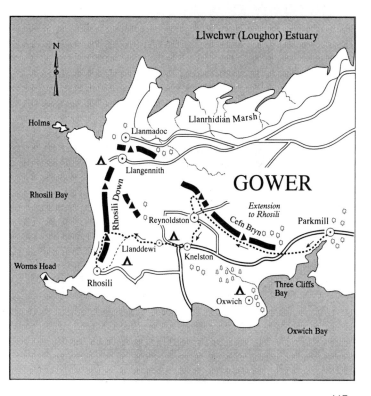

secluded Brandy Cove, where images of smuggling are conjured up. The path continues into Pwlldu Bay. Pwlldu Head rears up from the ocean and the twisting, wooded Bishopston Valley, which threads inland from an almost white limestone-pebbled storm beach.

A cottage by a small bridge over the Bishopston stream is passed on a path which rises steeply towards Pwlldu Head. On further ascent, views eastwards along the coastline to The Mumbles can be seen beyond the pastures that crown the limestone cliffs. To the south on a clear day the huge cliffs of Exmoor and the North Devon Coast can clearly be spied across the Bristol Channel.

At the top of the headland from the farm of High Pennard a path traverses fields on a southerly course to the promontory's edge. It then descends to a bracken-cloaked shelf still high above the shoreline and where a narrow path climbs once more to top the pale cliffs.

The path then descends to Deep Slade, a depression that briefly interrupts the magnificent limestone scenery, and, after ascending to the Southgate Lane west of Hunt's farm, the high clifftop path is resumed. The strata that form this next group are folded so that they are inclined upwards at 45 degrees from the sea shore. Mitchin Hole, situated in High Tor, is Gower's largest coastal cave. Following extensive excavations the bones of elephants, rhinoceros, hyena and humans have been discovered here.

Southgate is a small village which has been much enlarged in modern times to meet the commercial demands of this popular area, but its shops and hotel offer much needed refreshment - a notable feature on a hot day being the general store's large selection of ice-creams. Beyond the village is the delightful little cove, Pobbles Bay, where wide sandy beaches stretch to Oxwich 3 miles to the west. Jutting out in this expanse are the famous conical bluffs of Three Cliffs Bay and in the view further west rising from the fields of Penmaen is the whaleback sandstone escarpment of Cefn Bryn. Cefn Bryn is to Gower what the Pennines are to England.

Our entry to Three Cliffs Bay from Pobbles is over sandy terrain and skirts the Southgate Golf Links. This sheltered inlet is the estuary of Penard Pill, a narrow stream which meanders on the flat green floor of the valley which twists amongst the woodlands of Parkmill. When the tide is out the best course would be to walk on the beach under the arch in the Three Cliffs, otherwise a track on the western edge of Pennard Burrows is used.

The way continues along the east side of the estuary, passing the ruins of Penard Castle and its neighbouring ruined church.

The thirteenth century castle was built by the conquering Normans overlooking cliffs and steep slopes above the pill. It appears in few historical records, although one in 1650 records it as being 'desolate and ruinous'. The castle has always been dogged by sand encroachment and to this day known remnants remain buried for their own preservation.

In a final woodland approach to Parkmill a sharp descent is made to the Pill which is crossed at GR 545892 before reaching the A4118, where there is a convenient cafe. It will hardly seem like a fortnight and 200 miles since Llanfairfechan was left behind. The route has passed through some of the very best Wales has to offer, from the beautifully sculptured mountains of Snowdonia and lonely rolling moors of the Elenydd to the huge dams at Elan and Brianne. The mountains and their perennial elements will almost certainly have tested the spirit and resolve, but those who completed the journey over the Black Mountain and through the suburbs of Swansea to this final section above Gower's cliffs will go home far richer for the experience of a Welsh Coast to Coast Walk.

But wait; isn't there a bit left?

EXTENSION FROM PARKMILL TO RHOSILI

I thought most walkers would have had enough of a good thing by now, but quite a few people have written to me saying they thought the walk should have ended at Worm's Head, Rhosili. Here we go. I think that a climb to Cefn Bryn would be preferable to an extended walk along the south coast; this way you'll see the whole of the Gower Peninsula beneath your feet.

From Parkmill either follow the lane through North Hills farm or the path on the western side of Pennard Pool to Penmaen at the foot of Cefn Bryn. This escarpment of old red sandstone, described as the backbone of Gower, will take you almost 5 miles to the heart of the peninsula. A spectacular scene, the whole of Gower unfolds before your eyes as you climb on an old green road over slopes of bracken and rushes. To the north it is more austere; there's the stark coastal marshes of Llanrhidian, the Llwchwr (Loughor) estuary and the scattering of lowland towns (Llanelli, Gorseinon and Pontardulais) framed by the bare Lliw hills of yesterday and the Black Mountain from the day before. In the opposite direction is the crazy coastline from the wide conurbations of Swansea to Rhosili. The wide blue drifts round a beautiful mosaic of pasture hedgerow and village. It all comes to an abrupt end on the upthrusts of Rhosili Down and Llanmadoc Hill, those last bastions of Gower and the finishing point for our route.

A little tarmac road straddles the hill - it's a viewpoint round here for less energetic tourists. If there is time it would be worth a detour to see Arthur's Stone, a neolithic tomb (about 2500 BC). The capstone is claimed to weigh over 25 tons. One legend has it that King Arthur flung it from the other side of the Llwchwr estuary when he found it in his shoe.

The green road continues south of the marked trig point and our route leaves it on the path down to Reynoldston, an important village at the centre of Gower. A cross-field footpath heads south-westwards to the road just short of Knelston. Follow the road then a lane to Llanddewi, a little hamlet with a small church and adjacent sixteenth-century manor house.

Our route aims for Rhosili Down along the Kingshall Lane track, part of a waymarked farm trail centred on the Gower Farm Museum, Lake farm. It runs through pleasing pastoral scenery to the very foot of the Down. Old Henllys farm, passed en route was built for the Mansell family and was almost certainly used to store contraband in bygone days. Claims were rife that there was an underground passage from here to Rhosili, a distance of over 2 miles.

If you've had enough, then farm tracks lead from the foot of the Down into Rhosili, but wouldn't it be worth summoning up the energy for one last climb to the Beacon? There are a couple of megalithic tombs, known as Sweyne's Houses, 1/2 mile north of the trig point. Some people believe that the Scandinavian sea lord Sweyne gave his name to Swansea.

Contrary to its lowly height Rhosili Down feels like a true mountain and the views are exhilarating. As the coastal breeze wraps around you, you look down on that perfect beach; even the waves ebb and flow in perfect symmetry and graceful arcs. Looking westwards you can survey the Carmarthenshire and Pembroke coastline. To the south you look down on Worms Head (a worm was a sea monster, not the earthworm variety). If the tide is in it will be an island, if it's out it will be connected to the mainland by dusky ribs of rock carrying a myriad glistening rockpools. Further afield you may be able to pick out Lundy Island and the Somerset coast.

When you're ready you can amble down to the shore at Rhosili. Maybe this land of the setting sun will be true to its name and those parting rays will be glimmering pink on the waves and across the darkening Carmarthenshire coastline.

FACT FILE

Distances and Time

Main route to Three Cliffs Bay (Parkmill)	9mls	14km	4-5 hours
Extension to Rhosili	9mls	14km	4-5 hours

Terrain
Promenade and clifftop path with some hill walking and lanes on the Rhosili extension

CAUTION: There are only 2½ hours on each tide cycle that a crossing to Worms Head can be made. Check with the coastguard before any attempt is made. It is also quite a rough walk.

Accommodation
Hotels and B&B in Caswell Bay, Southgate, Parkmill, Oxwich and Rhosili. Campsites in Oxwich, Llanddewi and Rhosili.

Tourist Information
Swansea Tel 01792 468321

WALES - ITS HISTORY

After nearly four hundred years of occupation the Romans were forced by the decline of their Empire to retire from Britain. The Celtic tribesmen were left to regroup and defend themselves against the waves of invaders that were to follow. In Wales they successfully repelled the Picts and Scots but in England they were defeated by the Saxons. This isolated Wales and from this time England and Wales developed, in terms of culture, as two nations.

In the seventh century the Anglo-Saxons made attempts to raid the Welsh. Edwin of Northumbria made the first foray, but the Welsh chief Cadwallon and his allies of Mercia repelled him. King Offa of Mercia then attacked Wales himself. After many years of fighting Offa's Dyke was constructed to mark the boundary between the two neighbours. Both sides respected the borders.

The ninth century brought the onslaught by the Viking marauders who regularly plundered the Welsh coast. Rhodri Mawr led the Welsh against them and resisted their raids, which became more sporadic and less intensive until they eventually ended two centuries later.

Rhodri Mawr became the first leader of all Wales. His grandson Hywel Dda (Hywel the Good), a Welsh Chief himself, became famous for his codification of the law. These laws were recognised throughout Wales until the reign of Henry VIII, though after Hywel's death in 949 the country generally returned to disunity and tribalism.

The harmony that had existed between England under Alfred the Great and Wales under Hywel Dda was not to continue after the defeat of England by William of Normandy at Hastings in 1066. William decided that an independent Wales was not to be tolerated and embarked on what was to become a titanic and protracted struggle. His soldiers were better armed than those of the Welsh and they made steady, if slow, advances into Welsh territories. Three Norman barons, who became the first in a long line of powerful and troublesome Marcher Lords, made the initial attacks. They were William FitzOsbern, Earl of Hereford, in the South; Roger of Montgomery in Central Wales and Hugh of Avranches who led the attack of North Wales.

Although stiff resistance was offered throughout the next century, the Cambrian Princes were gradually forced to retreat to the hills. When the Normans established themselves in an area they built small motte and bailey castles to garrison their troops. These wooden castles on raised ground were later replaced by more permanent stone fortresses. Around these the first Welsh towns and villages developed, where previously habitation had been scattered.

On the death of Henry I, who had been a notorious scourge of Wales, there was a period of disputed accession, and England's temporary weakness was exploited by a new Celtic hero, Owen Gwynedd, who extended his territories virtually to the walls of Chester. In the south lands were recaptured, although not on such a grand scale. The Norman stronghold centred on Pembrokeshire and the Gower was impenetrable.

Henry II took power over England but after an abortive attempt at an invasion via the Berwyn Mountains, he adopted an uneasy truce with Owen Gwynedd and his southern counterpart Rhys-ap-Gruffydd.

It is about this time that Rhys-ap-Gruffydd confirmed the grant for the construction of Strata Florida, the Cistercian monastery that was to become such a civilising influence on Central Wales. Rhys is also renowned for congregating the bards for the first Eisteddfod at Cardigan in 1177.

The beginning of the thirteenth century saw the rise to power of a new leader, Llewelyn, Prince of Gwynedd, later to become Llewelyn the Great. He noted that the tribalistic structure of the Welsh was inferior to the feudal system adopted by the English, which he was able to institute in his subsequent uniting of Wales, despite some opposition.

Richard I was a contemporary of Llewelyn and his preoccupation with the Holy Wars, combined with his brother John's problems with his barons, meant that the Welsh leader's quest for power proceeded without English hindrance. Llewelyn even married John's daughter Joan, thus attaining some degree of alliance.

The Magna Carta signed by King John promised to give back to Wales the territory that had been taken, and when John died his successor Henry III reluctantly recognised Llewelyn's power over all Wales. Llewelyn died in 1240, and after a brief reign by his son

Dafydd, his grandson Llewelyn-ap-Gruffydd proclaimed himself Prince of Wales, a title that Henry II acknowledged in the Treaty of Montgomery.

In 1272 Edward I became King of England. He was not tolerant of this independent land on his western borders. For his part, Llewelyn had become over-confident of his powers, for he had long since ceased to pay homage to the English crown, as he was bound to do by agreement. He had also agreed to marry Eleanor, daughter of the traitorous Simon de Montfort, who had led the rebellion that had captured and briefly imprisoned Henry III. Diplomatic relations deteriorated.

In 1277 Edward attacked and by the summer of that year all Wales, except Gwynedd and Anglesey from where Llewelyn ruled, was in English hands. When Edward sailed his fleet through the Menai Straits, thereby dividing the two remaining strongholds, Llewelyn was forced to accept defeat. In the treaty that followed, he forfeited his powers over South and Central Wales; his marriage to Eleanor de Montfort was forbidden, and he was again compelled to pay homage to the English throne.

Llewelyn's brother Dafydd broke the treaty when, in 1282, he attacked and captured Howarden. This inspired an uprising and Llewelyn was forced into the fray. Edward repeated the tactics of the previous encounter and again penned the rebels within Gwynedd. Llewelyn, with a small guard, slipped through the English line and endeavoured to gain support from the South. This initiative came to an abrupt end on the outskirts of Builth Wells, however, where Llewelyn was killed by an English knight. Dafydd was executed and Wales yet again lost its independence.

Edward built a series of powerful castles including Conwy, Harlech, Caernarfon and Beaumaris, all still standing proudly today. They must have presented an image of irresistible domination to the Welshmen of those times.

Following this subjugation the next few generations of Welsh warriors fought with the English in the battlefields of France. It is said that leeks, for so long the symbol of Welsh national pride, were picked and worn as trophies by the victorious Gwent Bowmen from the fields of Crecy.

Owain Glyndwr (Owen Glendower) was a respected citizen

who had a place at the English Court, and it came as a great surprise when, after a meeting with rebels at Glyndyfrdwy in 1400, he was declared Prince of Wales. Henry IV sent an army to quell the rebellion but, after a year of harsh anti-Welsh laws, the war escalated and Conwy was recaptured for Wales by the Tudors, a family who later in the century were to emerge as rulers of England. Glyndwr was victorious at Nant Hyddgant to the north of Pumlumon (Plynlimon) (see Chapter 6). He then took Aberystwyth and Harlech after defeating the powerful Marcher Lord, Edmund Mortimer. In 1404 Glyndwr, who was by now in control of most of Wales, set up a Welsh Parliament at Machynlleth and had himself officially crowned Prince of Wales.

In 1407, as the rebellion lost some impetus, Harlech was lost to the English under Henry V. By 1410 all was lost and Glyndwr withdrew into obscurity. The aftermath of this last Welsh uprising was devastating. Severe laws were introduced barring Welsh citizens from congregating in any numbers without prior permission. They were not allowed to hold municipal office. The lands of Glyndwr's rebels were seized by the crown, while others were forced to retreat from the incessantly looted towns and villages and attempted to forge new lives on the less hospitable moorlands.

In the thirty years that followed the battle of St Albans in 1455, England was divided by the Wars of the Roses, in which the Houses of Lancaster and York disputed the accession to the throne. The Yorkists led by Edward IV gained power in 1461, and of great significance to Wales in the following period were Edward's successful efforts to reduce the powers of the Marcher Barons, who had been particularly perfidious in their allegiances.

It might seem inconceivable that after centuries of oppression a Welshman would rule all England, but such a man, Henry Tudor, a direct descendant of Llewelyn the Great, had become leader of the House of Lancaster, being the grandson of John of Gaunt. His forced exile to Brittany ended when he landed at Milford Haven and marched northward to Machynlleth gathering an army of Welshmen. He confronted the Yorkist troops of Richard III at Bosworth Field, near Leicester. Victory was Henry's, and thus in the year of 1485 a Welshman was crowned King of England.

The Battle at Bosworth effectively ended the Wars of the Roses and Henry secured the peace by marrying a Yorkist, Elizabeth, daughter of Edward IV. The restrictions imposed on the Welsh by Henry IV were lifted, and ambitious Welshmen soon began to move into England. In an early reform, Henry set up the Council of Wales, based at Ludlow. This precursor of the present Welsh Office was an administrative body set up to carry out Privy Council orders and supervise the judicial system within the principality.

In 1509 Henry VIII succeeded his father to the throne. His acts of 1536 and 1543 officially united England and Wales. The Welsh Laws of Hywel the Good were replaced by English Law, although Wales was allowed to retain its own law courts. Exchequers were established at Carmarthen, Denbigh, and Brecon alongside the already functioning one at Caernarfon. Because of its proximity to England, Monmouth was attached to the Courts of Westminster. This, and the fact that the county received the slightly preferential treatment afforded to England, had the effect of gradually alienating Monmouthshire from the rest of the principality.

The language used in the law courts was English, and this led to the eventual decline in the use of the Welsh language, especially in the urban areas of the South. As a result English became the language of the gentry and the scholars, who played down their Welsh origins. They were asked, about this period, to adopt surnames, as the English had done, for reasons of identification. The Welsh way of adding the father's name was found unsatisfactory and so, for example, a man known as Twm ap Hywel (Tom, son of Hywel) would probably have been Anglicised to Tom Powell.

The Act of 1536 required each Welsh county to be represented in Parliament by a knight of the shire, and each shire town, with the exception of poverty stricken Harlech, had a burgess as its representative. The Marcher Lordships were abolished and replaced by the new counties of Denbigh, Montgomery, Radnor and Brecknock.

There was little Welsh resistance to the Reformation and even to the suppression of the monasteries, which had long ceased to contribute greatly to the local communities. Indeed, there were many cases of monks being prosecuted for criminal activities. Abbot Salisbury of Valle Crucis (Llangollen), for instance, was convicted of highway robbery, and a monk from Strata Florida was jailed for counterfeiting. This did little to endear the religious orders to the people. The lands held by the monasteries and the Roman Catholic Church were confiscated and sold to laymen, usually members of the local gentry.

In 1563 Elizabeth I commissioned Richard Davies, Bishop of St Davids, to translate from Latin to Welsh both the Bible and a book of prayer. He collaborated with a notable scholar, William Salesbury, to complete the works without the Old Testament. Twenty years later William Morgan published a complete Bible translation. It has been said that these works helped to preserve the real Welsh language and to prevent its degradation into dialects and eventual decline, as the people heard good Welsh spoken every time they attended church.

Although Wales was involved in the Civil War the effects on the principality were few, and most of the battles were over the border in England. Largely its people were supporters of the crown because of previous allegiances to the Tudors.

Until the end of the sixteenth century the principality had been almost entirely pastoral. Now there was increased activity in the exploitation of minerals. Lead was found in abundance in Cardiganshire and the mines brought prosperity for the area. The large demand for timber as a fuel and to make ships rapidly diminished the Welsh forests, and the need for coal as an alternative fuel became evident. Coal was mined at this time in the coastal areas of Glamorgan, Carmarthenshire, Pembrokeshire and Flintshire and much of it was exported to Ireland and France. The seeds of industrialisation were sown.

By the eighteenth century the established church had become remote from the problems of the average Welshman. The Bishops elected were entirely English, many of them totally uninterested in their sees, and thus it was that Welsh Presbyterianism began to take root. At first the pioneers of Methodism remained within the framework of the orthodox church, but in 1811 the break did come, with eight Calvinist Methodists being ordained at Bala and thirteen at Llandeilo. The movement's success, which was largely due to the fiery enthusiasm of early pioneers, is very evident, for within the Welsh towns and villages their austere chapels outnumber the traditional parish churches.

The industrial revolution came a little later to Wales than to England. The mountains of Glamorgan and West Monmouthshire were rich in coal, iron ore and limestone, which made them ideal centres for iron making. In 1759 the Dowlais Iron Works in Merthyr Tydfil, which was to become the largest in the world, was established, soon to be followed by others at Ebbw Vale, Tredegar and Blaenafon.

The building of the railways proved to be the catalyst in the growth of the South Wales coalfields, and peaceful valleys became scarred with the black tips and winding gear of the pits, towering above the lines of terraced miners' cottages. These mines attracted Welshmen from the rural areas, which were starved of employment, initiating a shift in the population to urban communities.

In North Wales, slate-quarrying had become a major industry. The grey terraced towns of Llanberis, Blaenau Ffestiniog and Bethesda grew as their mountains were reduced and disfigured by the ravages of an industry that was as tough on its workers as on the landscape. Death and serious injury were commonplace within these communities.

After an economic boom during the Napoleonic Wars, the nineteenth century held much tribulation for Wales. Its industries went into decline and those who held a job were grossly underpaid, overtaxed and exploited. It was in this climate that the violent Chartist riots of the 1830s took place. The worst conflict occurred at Merthyr Tydfil, where twenty-seven were killed and seventy were injured, including twenty soldiers.

There was also trouble in rural areas where local communities rebelled against the owners of the turnpike roads who demanded a toll for passage. The toll-gates on these roads were the targets of the Rebecca Rioters. They had become a symbol of oppression to the impoverished hill farmers and tinkers. The name Rebecca came from the book of Genesis which said, 'And they blessed Rebekah and said unto her, thou art our sister, be thou the mother of thousands of millions and let thy seed possess the gate of those which hate them'. The rioters, dressed in female attire, destroyed the gates. Such was the degree of popular support for the Rebeccas that little information as to their identity was offered to the authorities.

In the second half of the century there was much activity by the newly formed trade unions who fought vehemently for workers' rights and wages in a period of strife that lasted to the turn of the twentieth century. Although there were successes, their militancy was sometimes their undoing, as in the Slate Miners' Strike of 1900-1903 where the workmen, spurred on by a previous victory, were forced to capitulate and return with no gains. The resulting lack in continuity of supplies had led to a search for alternative materials for the manufacture of tiles, and between 1898 and 1914 the workforce was halved.

Unfortunately there has been further exploitation of the Welsh countryside for new water schemes. The flooding of the Tryweryn Valley near Bala for Llyn Celyn resulted in the loss of a village and was received with massive protest, but to this day similar ventures are undertaken with little thought for the inhabitants.

The First World War brought about a great expansion in Welsh Industry. The government assisted the companies to increase productivity to meet the higher demands of wartime. By the conclusion of the war the coal mines of Belgium and France had been destroyed, thereby creating higher demand for Welsh coal. The period of prosperity lasted until 1923, when Wales sank into a depression which had afflicted much of the western world. This depression was to last longer in Wales than in other countries - until the Second World War, when it was made a development area, offering firms who moved there grants and incentives. Thus new industries were introduced to diversify the economy, which had previously failed so badly. Industrial estates such as the one at Fforest Fach, north of Swansea, were built, and gradually light industry has replaced the likes of coal and steel which decline to this day under the threat of cheap imports. The Forestry Commission, set up to remedy the lack of wood supplies following the First World War, was responsible for planting vast conifer forests not only in the rural areas but also in the redundant pit valleys.

In 1963 the Welsh Language Society was founded. Its objective was the equality of the Welsh and English Languages. They turned their attentions to the English road signs which they demanded should be bilingual, and in this they were successful, although their methods, such as the destruction of offending signs, were dubious.

Plaid Cymru, the Welsh Nationalist Party, won its first seat in

1966 and became a real threat to Labour's dominance in the 1970s, though its influence now seems to be receding. Its aim for a Free Wales seems unlikely and not universally supported amongst Welshmen, but it illustrates the fierce nationalism that has re-emerged and maybe in such a climate the cultures and idiosyncrasies of this nation will survive the eroding influences of time.

PLANNING THE TRIP

DISTANCE CHART	MAIN ROUTE miles (Km) stage	cum. total	MOUNTAIN ROUTE miles (Km) stage	cum. total
Llanfairfechan	0	0	0	0
Roewen YH	6 (9)	6 (9)	-	-
Drum	5 (8)	5 (8)	5 (8)	5 (8)
Carnedd Llewelyn	-	-	4 (6)	9 (14)
Helyg	9 (14)	14 (22)	3 (5)	12 (19)
Ogwen Cottage YH	-	-	3 (5)	12 (19)
Pen y Gwryd	4 (6)	18 (28)	-	-
Glyder Fawr	-	-	4 (6)	16 (25)
Pen y Pass	-	-	2 (3)	18 (28)
Yr Wyddfa (Snowdon)	-	-	3 (5)	21 (33)
Llyn Edno *1	5 (7)	23 (35)	-	-
Nantgwynant	8 (12)	25 (40)	4 (6)	25 39)
Llyn yr Adar *2	3 (5)	29 (45)	3 (5)	28 (44)
Moelwyn Mawr	-	-	2 (4)	30 (48)
Maentwrog	6 (10)	35 (55)	4 (6)	34 (54)
Trawsfynydd	6 (10)	41 (65)	6 (10)	40 (64
Nantcol	7 (12)	48 (77)	-	-
Rhinog Fawr	-	-	7 (11)	47 (75)
Barmouth	8 (13)	56 (90)	9 (15)	56 (89)
Kings YH (via Penmaenpool)	-	-	10 (16)	57 (91)
Penygadair (Cadair Idris)	-	-	8 (13)	64 (102)
Abergynolwyn	11 (17)	67(107)	6 (10)	70 (112)
Tarrenhendre	-	-	4 (6)	74 (118)

	MAIN ROUTE miles (Km) stage	cum. total	**MOUNTAIN ROUTE** miles (Km) stage	cum. total
Tarren y Gesail	-	-	4 (6)	77 (124)
Machynlleth	7 (11)	73 (118)	4 (7)	81 (131)
Pumlumon Fawr (Plynlimon)	-	-	11 (17)	92 (148)
Hafren Forest	-	-	3 (4)	95 (152)
Eisteddfa Gurig	16 (25)	89 (143)	-	-
Pant Mawr	6 (10)	95 (153)	5 (8)	100 (161)
Dyffryn Castell (from Pumlumon)-		-	*4 (6)*	*98 (158)*
Flickering Lamp				
(Penygarreg Dam)	14 (22)	110 (177)	14 (22)	114 (183)
Elan Village	2 (4)	112 (181)	2 (4)	116 (187)
Rhayader	*2 (3)*	*114 (184)*	*2 (3)*	*115 (185)*
Abergwesyn	11 (18)	123 (199)	13 (20)	129 (207)
Bwlch-y-fin (nr Llyn Brianne)	6 (10)	129 (209)	6 (10)	135 (217)
Nant-y-Bai (via Doethie)	-	-	5 (8)	140 (225)
Nant-y-bai (via Dinas)	4 (6)	133 (215)	-	-
Rhandirmwyn	2 (4)	135 (219)	2 (4)	142 (229)
Cilycwm	4 (6)	139 (225)	4 (6)	146 (235)
Llandovery	5 (7)	144 (232)	5 (7)	150 (242)
Myddfai	3 (5)	147 (238)	3 (5)	153 (245)
Llanddeusant YH	6 (9)	153 (247)	6 (9)	159 (258)
Careg Yr Ogof	3 (5)	156 (252)	-	-
Bannau Brycheiniog	-	-	4 (6)	163 (262)
Cwm twrch Uchaf	7 (12)	163 (264)	-	-
Garreg Lwyd	-	-	6 (10)	169 (272)
Glanamman (Aman Valley)	-	-	6 (10)	175 (282)
Ammanford	-	-	*3 (5)*	*175 (282)*

	MAIN ROUTE		MOUNTAIN ROUTE	
	miles (Km) stage	cum. total	miles (Km) stage	cum. total
Coynant (Ceunant)	10 (16)	173 (280)	6 (10)	181 (292)
Pontardulais	4 (7)	177 (287)	4 (7)	185 (299)
Felindre	3 (5)	176 (285)	3 (5)	184 (297)
Black Pill (Swansea Bay)	11 (17)	187 (302)	11 (17)	195 (314)
Caswell Bay	4 (6)	191 (308)	4 (6)	198 (320)
Parkmill (Three Cliffs Bay)	6 (9)	197 (317)	6 (9)	204 (329)
Rhosili (Gower Extension)	12 (19)	209 (336)	12 (19)	216 (338)

places in italics are off-route accommodation centres
* 1 without the descent to Nantgwynant
* 2 including the descent to Nantgwynant

MAPS REQUIRED
OS Landranger 1:50,000 Nos 115, 124, 135, 147, 160 and 159.
These maps are good for general hillwalkers but are not as good as OS Outdoor Leisure and Pathfinder maps (1:25,000) which show field boundaries and greater detail. Unfortunately the number of maps and the price would be prohibitive.

A good compromise would be to take OS Leisure Maps 16/17 (one map), 18, 23 and 12 coupled with Landrangers 135, 147, 160 & 159. NB: A small part of the route at Llanfairfechan wouldn't be covered this way.

TRANSPORT
LLANFAIRFECHAN has a railway station on the North Wales coastal line and is also reached by bus (Crosville Wales Ltd, Imperial Buildings, Glan y Mor Road, Llandudno Junction, Gwynedd LL31 9RH. Crosville run services across much of Wales).

If you want to do a half of the walk only, MACHYNLLETH has a railway link to Shrewsbury, Aberystwyth and Porthmadog.

Buses run from PARKMILL, Gower, near Three Cliffs Bay, and RHOSILI to Swansea. SWANSEA has an Inter-City railway station and reasonable bus links to the rest of the United Kingdom.

Although I have split the main route into twelve sections it is not a recommended schedule for all. Experienced long-distance walkers would easily be able to cover these distances, some maybe quicker, but it is best to choose the itinerary to match your preferred pace.

It is advisable to book accommodation well in advance. This is especially true in the summer months when the smaller establishments quickly fill up. I have not compiled an accommodation list. Experience tells me that they are out of date too quickly. Contact the tourist information centres - they are always glad to help and will send an accommodation list.

When booking your accommodation it is always best to advise the landlord/lady that you are on foot and may be late arriving; that way they should not give your room to somebody else. My wife Nicola tells me to mention that it is good if they have a bath rather than a shower, even if it is across the passage. It is nice to have a good soak after a hard day on the fells.

TIME TO GO?

The best time to tackle Snowdonia to Gower is probably in June or July. Daylight hours are at their longest and the climate is milder with a greater likelihood of some sunshine.

Many long-distance walkers like to set off in May. Spring flowers are blooming in the meadows and the contrast between the rust-red bracken and the trees' new green foliage can be striking. But frost and snow is still possible at this time; campers would have to pack their bulkiest sleeping bags and extra warm clothes. High-mountain walkers may, at this time, need to consider taking their crampons and ice-axes to reach the Snowdonian tops. More often than not at this time of the year, the terrain hasn't quite dried out - there may be an added squelch to your walk.

In August and September it can be wet, though there are blackberries in the hedgerows and bilberries on the hills. In the winter months daylight hours are too limited to achieve much distance. Unless you are an experienced winter mountain walker it is better to stick to spring and summer.

EQUIPMENT AND SAFETY

I am not going to cover this section in detail as there are books such as Clive Tully's *Trail Walking Handbook* and Chris Townshend's *The Backpacker's Handbook* which cover the subject far better than I could. Magazine articles and reviews such as those in *Trail Walker* or *The Great Outdoors* are also useful.

The successful long-distance walker should be reasonably fit although you do not have to be in the first flush of youth or a marathon runner. Build up your fitness gradually. Try doing long day-walks, then a lengthy weekend itinerary, complete with the gear you expect to take on the main trip. It is no use planning a schedule of 15 miles a day on a long-distance walk if the most you have ever done before is 10; this will almost certainly lead to difficulties.

It is extremely important that all hillwalkers are fully practised in the use of map and compass. Their lives depend on it. If the mist comes down on the mountain it is essential that you know exactly where you are and the direction required to get safely off the mountain.

Make sure you take enough food and water - keep some additional emergency rations in the corner of the rucksack. The average adult male walker needs about 4,000 calories each day; far more than you would need for a day at the office. Many people eat a lot of sweet things but, although some sugar is good for fast-releasing energy, starchy foods containing complex carbohydrates are the most important. These are contained in the likes of bread and potatoes. Eat some fat too - nuts and dairy products etc.

You'll need plenty of water, especially on hot days when the body perspires a lot. It is very easy and very dangerous to become seriously dehydrated. Fast flowing mountain streams usually contain good fresh water, fit for drinking. You can buy water purification tablets for extra security though they add an unpleasant taste. Also check a short way upstream for anything untoward that could pollute the water supply - like a dead sheep.

Some water you just don't need - rain. Good waterproofs are

essential. Modern breathable fabrics such as those made with Goretex, Cyclone and Sympatex linings are generally regarded as the best. I do know some walkers, however, who prefer to go for the non-breathable types, which are much cheaper, lighter and more compact. Unfortunately the condensation that forms on the inside of the garments makes the wearer feel wet and uncomfortable when they are taken off. Remember, getting cold and wet will make you vulnerable to hypothermia, even outside the winter months.

Always have a spare set of dry clothes. It is as important for morale as for safety. Keep them dry by using a rucksack liner - whatever they say, no rucksack is waterproof. While we are on the subject of rucksacks, try not to economize too much if purchasing one. Comfort is important and an ill-fitting or poorly designed one will cause fatigue very quickly. You probably will not go far wrong with adjustable-back sacks made by reputable manufacturers such as Berghaus, Karrimor or Lowe. If you are camping, even with the lightest-weight tents and sleeping bags, you will need at least a 55 litre rucksack to fit everything in - 65 is best. If you are staying in B&Bs you may get away with a 45 litre sack.

Try to keep the load in your rucksack down to 30lb (13.5kg) if you're camping and less if your hostelling or using B&Bs.

If you are camping in the mountains make sure your tent is designed for that purpose. It is amazing how quickly weather can change at high altitudes and it's even more amazing how quickly it can demolish a 'low-level' tent. Ridge tents need A-poles for stability. More modern designs include geodesic dome tents with flexible poles and tunnel tents (not usually quite as stable in high winds).

Sleeping bags are rated in 'seasons'. A 1-2 season sleeping bag will suffice for late spring to early autumn. It would be uncomfortable if night-time temperatures came anywhere near 0°C. Conversely a heavy sleeping bag would be uncomfortably hot in even the English summer. A 3-4 seasons bag is good enough for most English conditions though a 5 season (I wonder what the fifth season is?) would be needed for a Cairngorm winter. Synthetic fillings such as hollow fibre are bulkier than their down equivalents but offer more insulation when wet.

Make sure you are fully equipped with strong boots and ones which have been 'worn in'. Lightweight 3-4 season leather ones are probably best; fabric boots are usable if they have a waterproof membrane such as Goretex or Sympatex - without this they will leak like a sieve and you would end up with bad blisters and numb feet like wrinkled kippers. Unless you're going to tackle Snowdonia to Gower when there's snow and ice around, do not go over the top with rigid 4-season mountain boots: they will cause fatigue and also erode the footpaths more quickly.

Finally, do not forget to pack some emergency medical supplies (plasters, bandages etc). There are plenty of good kits around - see your local 'outdoor' shop.

NOTES

NOTES

NOTES

CICERONE GUIDES

Cicerone publish a wide range of reliable guides to walking and climbing in Britain, and other general interest books.

LAKE DISTRICT - General Books
CONISTON COPPER A History
CHRONICLES OF MILNTHORPE
A DREAM OF EDEN -Lakeland Dales
EDEN TAPESTRY
THE HIGH FELLS OF LAKELAND
KENDAL A SOCIAL HISTORY
LAKELAND - A taste to remember (Recipes)
LAKELAND VILLAGES
LAKELAND TOWNS
LAKELAND PANORAMAS
THE LAKERS
THE LOST RESORT? (Morecambe)
LOST LANCASHIRE (Furness area)
REFLECTIONS ON THE LAKES
AN ILLUSTRATED COMPANION INTO LAKELAND

LAKE DISTRICT - Guide Books
THE BORDERS OF LAKELAND
BIRDS OF MORECAMBE BAY
CASTLES IN CUMBRIA
CONISTON COPPER MINES Field Guide
THE CUMBRIA CYCLE WAY
THE EDEN WAY
IN SEARCH OF WESTMORLAND
SHORT WALKS IN LAKELAND-
 1: SOUTH LAKELAND
 2:NORTH LAKELAND
SCRAMBLES IN THE LAKE DISTRICT
MORE SCRAMBLES IN THE LAKE DISTRICT
THE TARNS OF LAKELAND VOL 1 - WEST
THE TARNS OF LAKELAND VOL 2 - EAST
WALKING ROUND THE LAKES
WALKS IN SILVERDALE/ARNSIDE
WESTMORLAND HERITAGE WALK
WINTER CLIMBS IN THE LAKE DISTRICT

NORTHERN ENGLAND (outside the Lakes
BIRDWATCHING ON MERSEYSIDE
CANAL WALKS Vol 1 North
CANOEISTS GUIDE TO THE NORTH EAST
THE CLEVELAND WAY & MISSING LINK
THE DALES WAY
DOUGLAS VALLEY WAY
WALKING IN THE FOREST OF BOWLAND
HADRIANS WALL
 Vol 1 The Wall Walk
 Vol 2 Walks around the Wall
HERITAGE TRAILS IN NW ENGLAND
THE ISLE OF MAN COASTAL PATH
IVORY TOWERS & DRESSED STONES (Follies)
THE LANCASTER CANAL
LANCASTER CANAL WALKS
A WALKERS GUIDE TO THE LANCASTER CANAL
WALKS FROM THE LEEDS-LIVERPOOL CANAL
LAUGHS ALONG THE PENNINE WAY
A NORTHERN COAST-TO-COAST
NORTH YORK MOORS Walks
ON THE RUFFSTUFF 84 Bike rides in Northern England

THE REIVERS WAY (Northumberland)
THE RIBBLE WAY
ROCK CLIMBS LANCASHIRE & NW
THE TEESDALE WAY
WALKING IN COUNTY DURHAM
WALKING IN LANCASHIRE
WALKING DOWN THE LUNE
WALKING IN THE SOUTH PENNINES
WALKING IN THE NORTH PENNINES
WALKING IN THE WOLDS
WALKS IN THE YORKSHIRE DALES (3 VOL)
WALKS IN LANCASHIRE WITCH COUNTRY
WALKS IN THE NORTH YORK MOORS (2 VOL)
WALKS TO YORKSHIRE WATERFALLS (2 vol)
WATERFALL WALKS -TEESDALE & THE HIGH PENNINES
WALKS ON THE WEST PENNINE MOORS
WALKING NORTHERN RAILWAYS (2 vol)
THE YORKSHIRE DALES A walker's guide

DERBYSHIRE PEAK DISTRICT & EAST MIDLANDS
KINDER LOG
HIGH PEAK WALKS
WHITE PEAK WAY
WHITE PEAK WALKS - 2 Vols
WEEKEND WALKS IN THE PEAK DISTRICT
THE VIKING WAY
THE DEVIL'S MILL / WHISTLING CLOUGH (Novels)

WALES, WELSH BORDER & WEST MIDLANDS
ASCENT OF SNOWDON
THE BRECON BEACONS
WALKING IN CHESHIRE
THE CHESHIRE CYCLE WAY
CLWYD ROCK
HEREFORD & THE WYE VALLEY A Walker's Guide
HILLWALKING IN SNOWDONIA
HILL WALKING IN WALES (2 Vols)
THE MOUNTAINS OF ENGLAND & WALES Vol 1 WALES
WALKING OFFA'S DYKE PATH
THE RIDGES OF SNOWDONIA
ROCK CLIMBS IN WEST MIDLANDS
SARN HELEN Walking Roman Road
SCRAMBLES IN SNOWDONIA
SEVERN WALKS
THE SHROPSHIRE HILLS A Walker's Guide
SNOWDONIA WHITE WATER SEA & SURF
WALKING DOWN THE WYE
A WELSH COAST TO COAST WALK
WELSH WINTER CLIMBS

SOUTH & SOUTH WEST ENGLAND
WALKING IN CORNWALL
WALKING IN THE CHILTERNS
COTSWOLD WAY
COTSWOLD WALKS (3 VOLS)
WALKING ON DARTMOOR
WALKERS GUIDE TO DARTMOOR PUBS
WALKING IN DORSET
EXMOOR & THE QUANTOCKS
THE GRAND UNION CANAL WALK
THE KENNET & AVON WALK
LONDON THEME WALKS
AN OXBRIDGE WALK
A SOUTHERN COUNTIES BIKE GUIDE
THE SOUTHERN-COAST-TO-COAST
SOUTH DOWNS WAY & DOWNS LINK
SOUTH WEST WAY - 2 Vol
THE TWO MOORS WAY Dartmoor-Exmoor
WALKS IN KENT Bk 2
THE WEALDWAY & VANGUARD WAY

SCOTLAND
THE BORDER COUNTRY - WALKERS GUIDE
BORDER PUBS & INNS A Walker's Guide
CAIRNGORMS WINTER CLIMBS
WALKING THE GALLOWAY HILLS
THE ISLAND OF RHUM
THE ISLE OF SKYE - A Walker's Guide
THE SCOTTISH GLENS (Mountainbike Guide)
 Book 1:THE CAIRNGORM GLENS
 Book 2 THE ATHOLL GLENS
 Book 3 THE GLENS OF RANNOCH
 Book 4 THE GLENS OF TROSSACH
SCOTTISH RAILWAY WALKS
SCRAMBLES IN LOCHABER
SCRAMBLES IN SKYE
SKI TOURING IN SCOTLAND
TORRIDON A Walker's Guide
WALKS from the WEST HIGHLAND RAILWAY
WINTER CLIMBS BEN NEVIS & GLENCOE

REGIONAL BOOKS UK & IRELAND
THE ALTERNATIVE PENNINE WAY
THE ALTERNATIVE COAST TO COAST
LANDS END TO JOHN O'GROATS CYCLE GUIDE
CANAL WALKS Vol.1: North
LIMESTONE - 100 BEST CLIMBS
THE PACKHORSE BRIDGES OF ENGLAND
THE RELATIVE HILLS OF BRITAIN
THE MOUNTAINS OF ENGLAND & WALES VOL 1 WALES, VOL 2 ENGLAND
THE MOUNTAINS OF IRELAND
THE IRISH COAST TO COAST WALK

Also a full range of EUROPEAN and OVERSEAS guidebooks - walking, long distance trails, scrambling, ice-climbing, rock climbing.

Other guides are constantly being added to the Cicerone List.
Available from bookshops, outdoor equipment shops or direct (send s.a.e. for price list) from
CICERONE, 2 POLICE SQUARE, MILNTHORPE, CUMBRIA, LA7 7PY

CICERONE GUIDES

Cicerone publish a wide range of reliable guides to walking and climbing abroad

FRANCE, BELGIUM & LUXEMBOURG
CHAMONIX MONT BLANC - A Walking Guide
THE CORSICAN HIGH LEVEL ROUTE: GR20
FRENCH ROCK
THE PYRENEAN TRAIL: GR10
THE RLS (Stevenson) TRAIL
ROCK CLIMBS IN BELGIUM & LUXEMBOURG
ROCK CLIMBS IN THE VERDON
TOUR OF MONT BLANC
TOUR OF THE OISANS: GR54
TOUR OF THE QUEYRAS
WALKING THE FRENCH ALPS: GR5
WALKING THE FRENCH GORGES (Provence)
WALKS IN VOLCANO COUNTRY (Auvergne)
THE WAY OF ST JAMES: GR65

FRANCE / SPAIN
WALKS AND CLIMBS IN THE PYRENEES
ROCK CLIMBS IN THE PYRENEES

SPAIN & PORTUGAL
ANDALUSIAN ROCK CLIMBS
BIRDWATCHING IN MALLORCA
COSTA BLANCA CLIMBS
MOUNTAIN WALKS ON THE COSTA BLANCA
WALKING IN MALLORCA
WALKS & CLIMBS IN THE PICOS DE EUROPA
THE WAY OF ST JAMES: SPAIN
WALKING IN THE ALGARVE

FRANCE / SWITZERLAND
CHAMONIX TO ZERMATT The Walker's Haute Route
THE JURA - Walking the High Route and Winter Ski
     Traverses

SWITZERLAND
THE ALPINE PASS ROUTE
THE BERNESE ALPS
CENTRAL SWITZERLAND
THE GRAND TOUR OF MONTE ROSA (inc Italy)
WALKS IN THE ENGADINE
WALKING IN TICINO
THE VALAIS - A Walking Guide

GERMANY / AUSTRIA / EASTERN EUROPE
HUT-TO-HUT IN THE STUBAI ALPS
THE HIGH TATRAS
THE KALKALPEN TRAVERSE
KING LUDWIG WAY
KLETTERSTEIG - Scrambles
MOUNTAIN WALKING IN AUSTRIA
WALKING IN THE BLACK FOREST
WALKING IN THE HARZ MOUNTAINS
WALKING IN THE SALZKAMMERGUT

ITALY & SLOVENIA
ALTA VIA - High Level Walks in the Dolomites
CLASSIC CLIMBS IN THE DOLOMITES
THE GRAND TOUR OF MONTE ROSA inc Switzerland))
ITALIAN ROCK - Rock Climbs in Northern Italy
VIA FERRATA - Scrambles in the Dolomites
WALKING IN THE DOLOMITES
WALKS IN THE JULIAN ALPS

MEDITERRANEAN COUNTRIES
THE ATLAS MOUNTAINS
CRETE: Off the beaten track
THE MOUNTAINS OF GREECE
THE MOUNTAINS OF TURKEY
TREKS & CLIMBS IN WADI RUM, JORDAN
THE ALA DAG - Climbs & Treks (Turkey)

OTHER COUNTRIES
ADVENTURE TREKS - W. N. AMERICA
ANNAPURNA TREKKERS GUIDE
CLASSIC TRAMPS IN NEW ZEALAND
MOUNTAIN WALKING IN AFRICA 1: KENYA
ROCK CLIMBS IN HONG KONG
TREKKING IN THE CAUCAUSUS
TREKKING IN NEPAL
TREKKING - WESTERN NORTH AMERICA

GENERAL OUTDOOR BOOKS
THE ADVENTURE ALTERNATIVE
FAMILY CAMPING
FIRST AID FOR HILLWALKERS
THE HILL WALKERS MANUAL
LIMESTONE -100 BEST CLIMBS IN BRITAIN
MOUNTAIN WEATHER
MOUNTAINEERING LITERATURE
MODERN ALPINE CLIMBING
MODERN SNOW & ICE TECHNIQUES
ROPE TECHNIQUES IN MOUNTAINEERING

CANOEING
CANOEIST'S GUIDE TO THE NORTH EAST
SNOWDONIA WILD WATER, SEA & SURF
WILDWATER CANOEING

CARTOON BOOKS
ON FOOT & FINGER
ON MORE FEET & FINGERS
LAUGHS ALONG THE PENNINE WAY
THE WALKERS

*Also a full range of guidebooks
to walking, scrambling, ice-climbing,
rock climbing, and other adventurous
pursuits in Britain and abroad*

*Other guides are constantly being added to the Cicerone List.
Available from bookshops, outdoor equipment shops or direct (send for price list)
from CICERONE, 2 POLICE SQUARE, MILNTHORPE, CUMBRIA, LA7 7PY*

PRINTED BY
CARNMOR PRINT & DESIGN, LONDON ROAD, PRESTON, U.K.